OF BORDERS AND MARGINS

Recent titles in

AMERICAN ACADEMY OF RELIGION
ACADEMY SERIES

SERIES EDITOR
Carole Myscofski, Illinois Wesleyan University

A Publication Series of
The American Academy of Religion and
Oxford University Press

Of Borders and Margins

Hispanic Disciples in Texas,
1888–1945

DAISY L. MACHADO

UNIVERSITY PRESS

2003

OXFORD
UNIVERSITY PRESS

Oxford   New York
Auckland   Bangkok   Buenos Aires   Cape Town   Chennai
Dar es Salaam   Delhi   Hong Kong   Istanbul   Karachi   Kolkata
Kuala Lumpur   Madrid   Melbourne   Mexico City   Mumbai   Nairobi
São Paulo   Shanghai   Taipei   Tokyo   Toronto

Copyright © 2003 by The American Academy of Religion

Published by Oxford University Press, Inc.,
198 Madison Avenue, New York, New York 10016

www.oup.com

Oxford is a registered trademark of Oxford University Press

Library of Congress Cataloging-in-Publication Data
Machado, Daisy L.
Of borders and margins : Hispanic Disciples in Texas, 1888–1945 / Daisy L. Machado.
p. cm. — (American Academy of Religion academy series)
Includes bibliographical references and index.
ISBN 0-19-515223-9
1. Hispanic Americans—Religion—Texas—History—20th century.
2. Disciples of Christ—Texas—History—20th century.
I. Title.   II. Series.
BX7318.5.H57 M22 2002
286.6'764'08968—dc21   2002025817

1 3 5 7 9 8 6 4 2

Printed in the United States of America
on acid-free paper

Para Mis Padres,
Y para Ismael . . . Y para
Todo nuestro pueblo que vive en los márgenes
y desde allí aman y sirven a Dios.

Preface

This is the history of the first Hispanic Disciples in the North American denomination known as the Christian Church (Disciples of Christ). The fact that those first Hispanic Disciples were from Texas makes the narration of this history one that must consider a series of external nonreligious forces. Why? Because this is the history of a denomination that was, in a very real sense, born and bred in the North American frontier. A denomination that because of this historical reality was necessarily shaped by the many forces—political, social, racial, economic—that were at work throughout the mid-nineteenth century in creating what is today Texas and the United States of America.

The Disciples of Christ moved into Texas in the mid-nineteenth century following that human river of western settlers who were in search of land. In Texas the Disciples sought to serve the Anglo settlers but also came face-to-face with the Tejanos who had already lived in that territory for generations. How Disciples ministered to the Tejano "other," as well as their mission focus and work among the Tejanos is what this book seeks to tell. But more than just a description of events and new church starts, this research project also seeks to give an explanation for why the Disciples could not create a successful ministry among Tejanos. This failure is still evident today as the Hispanic population in the United States steadily increases and the Disciples find themselves at a loss to respond effectively. This inability to respond to a changing world, in which race and ethnicity become more diverse and yet are necessary factors in the growth of any denomination in the United States, can be traced to a past in which the Disciples did little to reach beyond their racially comfortable congregations. They did little to prepare Hispanic clergy in Texas and invested even less in the area of church starts throughout the growing Hispanic communities of Texas.

This is a telling of history from a "margins" perspective. What this means is that the historical data is interpreted from the Hispanic perspective and not from the viewpoint of the denominational bureaucracy. That is why in order to tell this history from a perspective that is not the dominant one, I have found it is necessary to place the history of the Disciples in Texas within the larger context of the history of the United States. This means that I take into account the forces involved in the creation of both a nation and a state, forces that may be overlooked or considered either historically commonplace or even insignificant. I do this not to make this book "politically correct." or to try my hand at "revisionist history." Instead, the examination of this history from my particular lens or perspective is an effort to give voice or to call attention to issues and concerns that are not just abstract ideas or mere historical data but have taken flesh by becoming today's realities. These are realities shaped by a past that lives on in the present and continues to affect Hispanic Disciples living in the United States.

The forces examined in this historical analysis are relations with Mexico in the mid-to-late nineteenth century, the colonization and annexation of Northern Mexico by Euro-Americans into what is today Texas, the economics of the slave issue, the concept of manifest destiny, and especially the issue of race, which is a crucial piece of this history. The reader will note that the Spanish *conquista* of the sixteenth century does not play a major role in this historical narrative for two main reasons: (1) my analysis begins more than three centuries after the arrival of the Spaniards in Mexico, which means that the empire of Nueva España has already taken root, creating a new mestizo society, a new world order, that had emerged from the violent union of the Spanish and the indigenous; and, (2) the revolution for freedom from the Spanish yoke had also begun during this time, creating new political, economic, and social changes that would give birth to a new society whose dynamics would be very different from the one preceding it. Therefore, the Euro-Americans who entered the eighteenth-century northern borderlands of the empire of Nueva España were not encountering the postconquest society of the sixteenth century, nor coming into contact with a colonized people who stood with their heads bowed to Spain. This history unfolds on a different stage, yet the struggles between church and state have not been resolved so they continue to be important for the telling of this history, especially when the United States is introduced as a third player, bringing Protestantism as a new element to the story. Therefore, one cannot separate these external forces from the history of the Disciples in Texas. This is especially true because the boundaries between church and state were often blurred as church sought to serve state in the creation of what many in the newly emerging United States believed was to be a new nation blessed with God's particular favor.

The story of the encounters of the borderlands people of Texas with Austin and with other North American settlers, including the Disciples of Christ, is indeed a complex one. The first chapter seeks to examine the layers of meaning behind the history of this encounter between mestizo Tejanos and Euro-Americans. The second chapter will look at the ideologies about the frontier that were held by North American settlers. The third chapter will explore the creation of the Disciples of Christ—its identity, theology, and its relation to the frontier it sought to christianize. The fourth chapter will look at colonial and Mexican Texas and the impact of the arrival of the North American Protestant settlers who "re-made" Texas into an exclusive frontier. And the fifth chapter will close with an examination of the nineteenth-century Texas Disciples themselves and what their work with the Tejanos they encountered was all about.

The telling of this history is possible because of many people. First to Dr. Martin Marty, a special word of thanks for seeing value in this project; his affirmation was a sign of hope. And second because the telling of this history is done from the margins, that is, from the experience of an ordained Hispanic Disciples woman who belongs to a wider faith community, this is clearly not my history alone. It is also the history of today's Hispanic Disciples, laity and clergy, who face the past and yet continue to serve and worship in the Disciples denominational body and who do so with fidelity, love, and great hope for the future. To these: The Reverend David Vargas, prophet and friend, *¡gracias Druby!* To the members of the Latino congregations I have served, to my colleagues who serve our Latino Disciples congregations, and finally to those who are today's *Discípulos hispanos, ¡continuamos la lucha!*

And to my many Euro-American Disciples friends, laity, clergy, and seminarians, we will continue to minister together, to believe in and therefore work to make a reality the Disciples ideal that, "Transcending all barriers within the human family such as race and culture, the church manifests itself in ordered communities of disciples bound together for worship, for fellowship and for service."[1]

Contents

Note on Usage

The telling of a national history is really about power and exclusion. This is so because history is the telling of a story told by those who had the power to impose themselves. It is not surprising then, that those who hold the power to tell their story also hold the power to name themselves and exclude others from that self-definition. In the historical narrative that you are about to read I have made a distinction between the United States, whose people have chosen to call themselves "American" and their country "America," and all the other people who also make up the Americas. I have done this to keep present for the reader the reality of power and exclusion, which are important sub-texts to the overall story I have written. I have therefore decided to use the term "North America" to refer specifically to the United States and "North American" to refer to a person from the United States. I use this terminology instead of using the commonly accepted name "America" or "American." I have done this because I believe that in the Western Hemisphere there is not just one America and not just one specific type of American. I hold that in the western hemisphere there are other Americas—including Central America, Latin America, Caribbean America—which have historically been categorized, and continue to be categorized or defined, as other than and/or not American.

The creation of this distinction has come to us by a very long and complex process of nation building, national mythologies, and economic, political, and military expansionism combined with racial categorization. Because history in the service of nation building has been an important tool in this process and is an important component of the history I am examining, I offer the reader an opportunity to use another paradigm in which the power of names and self-naming do not go unexamined or ignored.

OF BORDERS AND MARGINS

The Making of a Nation

The Significance of the Texas Borderlands

Nueva España—Colonial New Spain

Texas, a land of vast expanses, defies a single broad vision of its past. . . .
Furthermore, the land has attracted a variety of immigrants, ranging
from the first Indian settlers, to Spaniards, Mexicans, people from the
United States, and Europeans from several nations.[1]

Within the complex history of Texas can be found the Christian Church
(Disciples of Christ), and to tell the history of the Christian Church in
Texas is to narrate a history on two levels. On one level, it is the history
of the westward expansion of the United States. On a second level, it is
an examination of the role and significance of the Texas borderlands, not
only for the United States, but also for the Disciples themselves. The Disciples of Christ movement came to Texas as a religious body born and
shaped in the expanding nineteenth-century western frontier of a nascent
United States. As such it was a uniquely North American[2] religious
movement. This means that when the Disciples of Christ settlers arrived
in Texas they carried with them North American ideologies and self-
definitions. However, as the Disciples settled in Texas they were further
influenced and shaped by the many realities and struggles of the particular borderlands territory they now called home. This is important to point
out because the racial and cultural realities of the Texas borderlands[3] and
the conflict these realities generated were part and parcel of the encoun-

3

ter between Euro-American frontier people and the borderlands people. When these are added to the political and economic factors also found in the borderlands, an ethos was created that greatly influenced the ministry of the Texan Disciples of Christ to and with the Mexican population. This influence and shaping were notable throughout the late nineteenth century, into the twentieth century, and exists up to the present day in Disciples ministry with the state's Hispanic/Latino[4] population.

What was this borderlands like? To begin to understand the Texas borderlands one must realize that it was shaped by the south-to-north movement of a people and culture that have not been included in the familiar east-to-west historical discourse of the United States. Texas, *las Floridas* (East and West Florida), and Louisiana, which was obtained by Spain from the French in the 1760s, served as a geopolitical borderlands for the colonial empire of Spain in the western hemisphere. The westward movement of North American pioneers took place in lands and territories whose pattern of culture and society was already formed by the Spanish.

This western frontier, so romanticized in the U.S. national epic, belonged to a population made up of different races whose worldview and self-understanding came into conflict with the incoming U.S. frontier settlers. This borderlands was Native American but it was also Spanish and Mexican. In this borderlands there could be found a variety of languages, religions, and cultures. Yet "[North] Americans have usually treated the westward movement as a human juggernaut that rolled relentlessly over Indian and Mexican as a vast and wonderful land was plundered in the name of progress."[5]

The tendency for U.S. history to be presented as a national drama of the ever advancing frontier population that bravely *conquered* the western *wilderness* has created a series of inconsistencies in our national historical discourse. It is a bias that persists to this day as the significance of the Spanish and Mexican influence in all the southwestern United States borderlands continues to be ignored. Take for example the statement made by T. R. Fehrenbach in his popular history *Lone Star: A History of Texas and the Texans*. The fact that Fehrenbach can state in a well-known history of the state that "the first successful Hispanic colonization of Texas was not to come until much later, in the 20th century"[6] points to the inconsistencies of our national historical memory. It is also an example of the arrogant ease with which the historical place and contributions of non-Caucasian people have been dismissed in our national narrative.

There exists a blatant disregard for the reality of a broader history not only for Texas but for the other southwestern borderlands as well.

And in this disregard there is a tacit denial of the relevance of an Ibero-American history that began as early as 1609 when the first Spanish settlement in North America was established in Santa Fe. Nationalistic historical sagas to the contrary, for over three centuries these southwestern borderlands belonged to both the people already there, as well as to the currents of people that traveled not east-to-west but south-to-north. Many of these people were nomadic Native Americans, others lived and hunted in the plains, or they came from Mexico and from the Caribbean into the North American borderlands.

The fact remains that the Spanish presence in and influence upon these same southwestern borderlands is one that cannot be dismissed or overlooked. The arrival of the Spaniards to the Americas in 1492 forever changed human history on both sides of the Atlantic Ocean. Not only did this encounter of races and cultures have the great economic consequences that Adam Smith examined in his book *The Wealth of the Nations*, but it created what anthropologists, like Olivia Harris[7] and others, have identified as myths about both the European explorers and the people they encountered. These myths were used for centuries to rationalize the conquest experience and to defend the conquerors. For example, Cristobal Colón and James Cook, European navigators and explorers, have been mythologized. Columbus is an icon of the Renaissance and Cook of the Enlightenment and as such both men represent two considerable European periods of "rebirth"and "awakening" that stand in contrast to the savageness and backwardness of the indigenous people they "discovered." What is being suggested here is that the arrival of the Europeans in the Americas attained an almost transcendental quality. However, inherent in that interpretation is the Spaniards' and other Europeans' conceptualization of self which necessarily created paradigms of difference in which the indigenous people were identified as inferior because of their race, religion, and culture.

What this means for the history of the borderlands is that the first violent and bloody sixteenth-century conquest perpetrated by the Spaniards was followed by a second conquest perpetrated by the United States in the nineteenth century. In each conquest the people indigenous to the land were assigned the category of inferior, and in each conquest religion and theological rationalizations were developed to justify the violence and aggression. In each conquest race was used as a paradigm to assign difference and worth. In each conquest the land became the stage for this human drama and it too was given divine or transcendental worth. Despite the importance and reality of the experience of the Spanish *conquista*, dating from the sixteenth century, for the purposes of this narrative, it does not really play a major role for two main reasons: (1) The historical analysis of this narrative begins more than three centuries after the arrival of the Spaniards in Mexico, which means that the empire of Nueva España had already taken root, creating the new mestizo society and a new world order; and, (2) the Spanish *conquista*, while undeniable in its bloody aftermath, was absorbed in the ongoing process of the creation of the empire of Nueva España.

Therefore the Euro-Americans who entered the eighteenth-century northern borderlands of the empire of Nueva España were not encountering the postconquest society of the sixteenth century. This history unfolds on a different stage, despite the similarity between the Spaniards' and Euro-Americans' self conceptualizations, despite the importance of race as a category used to assign worth, and the continued connection between church and state. This final element is especially important and plays an even more prominent role when the United States is introduced as a third player, which brings Protestantism as a novel and significant element to the history of the southwestern borderlands.

This means that in order to more clearly understand the role Texas played as part of the borderlands of the Spanish empire called Nueva España, a broader national and international picture must also be examined. This examination includes the many geographical maneuvers that took place, as well as the political players involved in the struggle to control this contested territory. Our historical narrative begins during the first forty years of the new republic of the United States. It was under the leadership of the first six presidents of the new republic (1789–1829), from Washington, Adams, Jefferson, to Madison, Monroe, and Quincy Adams, that early expansionist aspirations were both envisioned and realized. The administrations of these presidents helped to politically and militarily move the United States in the direction of creating a new transcontinental nation. Yet because their major obstacle for expansion to the south and west was Spain, the political posture assumed was that whether by diplomacy, threats, or military action, the North American advance toward the west was not going to be easily checked.

George Washington, president from 1789 to 1797, signed the first of many U.S. treaties with Spain, and each of which served to further open the door to the westward expansion of the new nation. The Treaty of San Lorenzo Escorial, signed on October 27, 1795, is known in U.S. history books as Pinckney's Treaty, and its focus was the use of the Mississippi River, a key waterway for both nations. Eleven years before the signing of the treaty, James Madison had declared his opinion on the matter in a letter to Thomas Jefferson, stating "'Nature' had given to the [North] Americans the navigation of the Mississippi."[8] This statement reflects one of the ideologies undergirding the westward expansion of the United States. In the case of the Mississippi River, Madison gave voice to what some historians have called the ideology of "geographical predestination." This ideology "held that nature or the natural order of things destined natural boundaries for nations in general and the United States, the nation of special destiny, in particular."[9]

It is not surprising then that the political diplomacy of Secretary of State Thomas Jefferson responded to this idea of geographical predestination. In the Treaty of Escorial, Jefferson was helping to fulfill this predetermined "right" of North Americans to freely navigate the Mississippi River. The treaty was a political, economic, and ideological victory: the United States secured from Spain duty-free navigation of the Mississippi by U.S. boats; the right to load and unload boats in New Orleans, which opened up a rich southern port to U.S. commerce; as well as the setting of 31 degrees as the northern border of West Florida. This last concession was of particular importance because it meant that Spain abandoned "its claim to the Ohio Valley and the one hundred mile strip below the Yazoo River."[10] In other words this treaty clearly marked "the beginning of Spain's retreat in the Mississippi Valley."[11]

The expansionist determination of these early leaders of the United States was also fueled by the interests of several economic sectors of the late eighteenth and early nineteenth centuries. For example, the westward expansion of the United States favored the economic interests of the southern plantation owners, the interests of the lucrative fur trade, as well as the interests of the developing northeastern manufacturers. But it was also used as a political platform predicated on an ideology of ethnocentric pride advanced by the idea of a national manifest destiny.

> Found within this manifest destiny are metaphysical dogmas of providential mission and quasi-scientific "laws" of national development, conceptions of national right and ideals of a social duty, legal rationalizations and appeals to "higher law," aims of extending freedom, and designs of extending benevolent absolutism.[12]

By the early nineteenth century Spain was facing its most formidable ideological, economic, and military foe. The newly independent United States had rapidly become more dangerous than England or France ever had been. Worst of all, the new nation was right on the eastern banks of Spain's rivers. Juan Gassiot, a member of the staff of the commander of the Interior Provinces for Nueva España in the 1780s, warned his colonial government about the United States' expansionist reputation and their westward moving pioneers. And Gassiot was not the only one. Vicente Manuel de Zéspedes, who was governor of East Florida (1784–1790) and who lived in San Augustine, described the North American frontiersmen as "nomadic like Arabs and . . . distinguished from savages only in their color, language, and the superiority of their depraved cunning and untrustworthiness."[13] Spanish colonial officials, and later officials of the newly formed Mexican nation, always mistrusted the motives and movement of the North American frontier population, but they quickly discovered there were other forces feeding the expansionist movement.

In addition to the strong manifest destiny ideology, the continuing economic and political development of the young United States also worked against Spain's empire in North America. The United States was not only a threat because it was geographically "next door," it was also becoming more aggressive in other key areas. Feeling threatened, Spain moved to adopt the defensive posture it had historically taken in Nueva España. In the past, when facing attacks against its empire, Spain used its northern borderlands as a geographical buffer to protect its wealth and influence to the south in Mexico City and beyond into Buenos Aires. But in the early 1800s the use of geographical borderlands to serve as a buffer against an expanding United States was no longer sufficient. There were three key factors in the early nineteenth century that tipped the scales and helped to accelerate the westward expansion of the United States. First of all, unlike England and France, the United States enjoyed the advantage of proximity and could quickly move its troops or easily enter into diplomatic negotiations. Spain would soon discover that the young nation was not hesitant about engaging in a military conflict. A second factor that worked against Spain was the growing population of the United States. By the 1820s the United States had a population of 9,600,000 compared to 6,200,000 in Nueva España.[14] A third threat was that this same population was one that was not easily contained within its borders. Spain quickly discovered that a real danger to the welfare of its colonial empire were the large numbers of North Americans who poured over the Appalachians in pursuit of territory and trade in the Mississippi Valley.[15]

The third and crucial factor was economic. Nueva España was the most prosperous of the Spanish colonies. It "had made remarkable strides in mining and commerce in the eighteenth century and boasted more millionaires than any other part of the hemisphere."[16] But by the nineteenth century it was in the United States that the great economic growth and vitality were taking place. By 1800, the economy of the agrarian United States was twice as productive as that of New Spain.[17]

Spain's response to the great economic and demographic gains of the United States was a defensive one, which produced new policies to curb the encroachment by its neighbor into its territories. An early but unsuccessful attempt was made to close the lower Mississippi to all but Spanish shipping in 1784. Then came the new immigration policies of the mid-1780s, which sought to promote the movement of new settlers directly from the Canary Islands into Nueva España at government expense. In an effort to let the North Americans clearly know they were on Spanish soil, immigration policies now required the Euro-American settlers who moved to las Floridas or Louisiana to take an oath of allegiance to Spain. But these policies became difficult to carry out.

Spain then departed from all prior diplomatic strategies and surprisingly initiated a series of alliances with the native peoples of Nueva España. The first of these alliances was with the Creeks, Choctaws, and Chickasaws in 1784 and later with the Comanches in Texas and Nuevo México in 1785 and 1786.[18] The Treaty of Nogales was signed in 1793 and "unified the major southeastern tribes into a confederation"[19] that was now aligned with Spain. These treaties were created for mutual assistance. They represented the tribal leaders' concern that their hunting land was being rapidly settled by North Americans and Spain's desire to maintain a buffer zone against United States expansionism.

Yet despite her endeavors to keep a tight control on Nueva España, Spain also faced situations in Europe that only served to further weaken her position in the western hemisphere. The inept monarchy of Carlos IV (1788–1808), compounded by the French Revolution and the Napoleonic Wars, all chipped away at Spain's power and finances. Another great geopolitical setback came when the ambitious but incompetent Manuel Godoy, who was also Carlos IV's chief advisor and Queen María Luisa's lover, sold the Louisiana territory to France in 1800. Meeting in secret negotiations, so that the United States would not intervene, Spain and France signed their sales agreement.

As an incentive to the sale of this territory to the French, the agreement included what Spain believed were two important promises. The first was that France would not sell the remaining territory of Louisiana to a third party, which seemed to help check the U.S. expansionist threat for Spain. The second was the promise that María Luisa's brother was to be given a throne in central Italy by Napoleon. However, much to Spain's dismay, Napoleon never fulfilled either promise. To make matters worse, because the agreement did not include formalized borders of the actual territory sold by Spain to France, in 1803 when Napoleon turned around and sold the Louisiana territory to the United States, Spain came out the true loser. Aware that the ambiguity of borders worked to the advantage of the United States, President Thomas Jefferson moved quickly to continue the expansionist agenda.

The first thing Jefferson did was to send troops to the edge of West Florida and there he threatened war. Only when convinced that military action would, in the words of one of his cabinet officers, "appear unjustifiable in the opinion of mankind and even of America," did the U.S. president back down just short of war.[20] In reality President Jefferson was claiming as U.S. territory a geographical area that had not been explored or mapped by the North Americans. Sensing the bargaining importance of knowing as much as possible about the Louisiana territory west of the Mississippi, Jefferson sought to be fully informed about these lands. To satisfy this need for official reconnaissance, two expeditions into the Louisiana territory were organized. The first was led by Meriwether Lewis and William Clark during the years 1804–1806 as they traveled up the Missouri River. The second took place in 1806 on the Red River and was led by Thomas Freeman and Peter Custis. Both of these expeditions were sponsored by President Jefferson and paid for with government funds.

Spain knew that her claim over the Louisiana territory was certainly lost, so what became of paramount importance was establishing clear boundaries to keep from losing any more of her North American holdings further to the west. Since Spain had already explored much of the Louisiana territory, the existing territorial archives became useful as Spain tried to build her case for the setting of the boundaries of the Louisiana territory. As added insurance the Spanish court commissioned "an elderly Mexican-born scholar, José Antonio Pichardo, [who] prepared a thirty-one-volume, 5,127-page report on "'The Limits of Louisiana and Texas.'"[21] This report eventually helped the Spanish negotiators as they attempted to settle the boundary question with the United States. However, the expansionist ambitions of the United States were becoming more and more forceful. Carlos Martínez de Irujo, Spain's minister to the United States, correctly understood that President Jefferson wanted to push America's border "up to the coasts of the South Sea [the Pacific]."[22] And move westward was exactly what Jefferson did.

In 1806 President Jefferson sent troops toward the Texas–Louisiana border. Tensions mounted as Lieutenant Colonel Simón Herrera, with his Spanish troops, and General James Wilkerson, commanding the U.S.

troops, faced one another. Bloodshed was averted by the astute dealings of these two experienced soldiers; the result of their stand-off was the Neutral Ground Agreement, which left the border question to be resolved by future diplomatic negotiation between the two governments. Meanwhile, the neutral zone became a notorious home to fugitive slaves, outlaws, smugglers, and squatters from the United States and a staging ground for filibustering expeditions into Texas.[23]

The presidency of James Madison, 1809–1817, not only continued the westward movement of the United States but was marked by blatant filibustering expeditions. Filibuster incidents in the early nineteenth century United States were plentiful. The earliest was probably in 1810 when the Euro-American residents of West Florida marched into Baton Rouge and declared the territory of West Florida an independent republic. They petitioned the Washington government for annexation and President Madison responded quickly. While he refused to recognize the rebel government, Madison did insist that West Florida, as far as the Perdido River, had belonged to the United States since 1803.[24] This claim on West Florida helped justify the incorporation of these lands, known as the "Florida parishes," in 1812 into what became the state of Louisiana.

East Florida was also the site for filibustering by Euro-Americans who "crossed the St. Marys River from Georgia, staged an uprising, formed the Republic of Florida, organized a provisional government, and took possession of . . . St. Augustine."[25] The leader of this operation was a U.S. army officer named General George Mathews, and the reason he failed was that in the "end he was disavowed by his government."[26] Yet when Mobile was captured by General Wilkerson in 1813, during the War of 1812, the city was never returned to Spain and was later incorporated into the new state of Alabama in 1817.

In a similar geopolitical maneuver the other adjacent territories were also incorporated into the new state of Mississippi. As President Madison pressed on with his ideal of creating a bi-coastal nation, filibuster activity seemed to reach an apogee. How much support Madison's administration gave to the filibusters is still a topic of debate, but one thing is certain, the filibusters were true agents of manifest destiny. It can also be said that their brazen military activities were ultimately beneficial to the Madison administration by helping to push Spain further and further south.

During the early nineteenth century the newspapers of the United States also became instruments for shaping and persuading public opinion in regards to the continuous westward movement of the United States. The journalism of this time greatly helped to fuel the expansionist fires of manifest destiny. As early as 1810 the *Boston Patriot*, in its October 8 issue, called for the freedom of Cuba, claiming it was under British influence and was a threat to United States security.[27] In December 1811 the Baltimore *Weekly Register* celebrated the filibuster activities of William Magee in Louisiana as he and other insurgents, who were Euro-Americans as well as Spanish republicans, declared their independence from Spain.[28]

In 1812 José Bernardo Gutiérrez de Lara, a well-known associate of Magee, went with Samuel Kemper and a group of Euro-Americans into Texas, declaring themselves the Republican Army of the North.[29] In the spring of 1813 the Lara-Kemper filibuster army captured San Antonio and proclaimed Texas an independent republic. This filibuster activity had received "tacit support and modest monetary aid from United States officials."[30] News of this event was publicized and applauded in the Leesburg, Virginia, *Genius of Liberty* on April 20, 1813, and also in Baltimore's *The Weekly Register* on July 17, 1813. The *Weekly Register* even went on to celebrate both the "complete annihilation of papal authority" in the new Texas republic and the movement of the people of Texas toward a "republican system of government" that would "avenge the death of Hidalgo."[31] Even the usually conservative Washington, D.C., *National Intelligencer* reported in their July 8, 1813, issue that the victory of the filibusters in San Antonio was proof "that a few hundred well chosen men were capable of penetrating into any part of New Spain," and that "Spain was incapable of resistance."[32]

The attack on San Antonio was the furthest south into Nueva España the filibusters had ever moved, and this time Spain responded with strong military action. Because "Texas had clearly resumed its historic position as a buffer province,"[33] Spanish forces quickly recaptured Texas from the filibusters in 1813 and "in a bloody purge, executed tejanos suspected of republican tendencies."[34] By the 1810s Spain found herself fighting on two fronts. Externally Spain was trying to stop United States expansionism, while internally Spain was facing the republican forces pushing for independence within its own empire. The external filibustering in West Florida, Louisiana, Texas, and Cuba, as well as the expansionist designs of the Washington government, were no longer its only concerns. In 1810 the city of Guanajuato, in the province of Querétaro, became another political sore spot within Nueva España. It was here that the clandestine meetings of a revolutionary group led by Father Miguel Hidalgo y Costilla were being held.

Like many of the native clergy, Father Hidalgo supported independence from Spain. On September 16, 1810, he rang the bell of the small church in the town of Dolores, raising the battle cry, "¡*Viva nuestra Señora de Guadalupe, viva la Independencia!*" Despite the eventual defeat and executions of the insurgent leaders, Mexico's revolution for independence from Spain was not to be stopped. This was made evident in the Constitution of 1814, known as the Constitution of Apatzingán, drafted by the insurgents who were now led by the priest José María Morelos y Pavón. Though it never had any vital force . . . [this Constitution] stands as . . . a monument to the incipient nationalism of México.[35]

It was under President James Monroe, 1817–1825, that the earlier claims that Texas was part of Louisiana and therefore belonged to the United States not only resurfaced but were politically settled in the Treaty of Adams-Onís. This treaty was signed in Washington, D.C., on February 22, 1819, by Secretary of State John Quincy Adams and the Spanish envoy Luis de Onís y González. In the treaty Spain "would cede East Florida to the United States and would tacitly recognize [North] America's de facto control of West Florida" and the United States would relinquish its claim to Texas.[36] The fact that the United States would now control West Florida was of vital importance "because it meant, as did control of New Orleans, command of the Mississippi."[37]

Clearly defined boundaries between the two nations were also established as a result of this treaty, though they were not formally agreed upon by both governments until twelve years later in 1832. The officially recognized boundaries between the United States and Nueva España ran along the Sabine River, which separates Texas and Louisiana, continued along the Red and Arkansas Rivers, then moved west along the 42nd parallel. Secretary of State Adams's vision of what the United States would ultimately look like became more tangible in the ratification of this treaty. He wrote, "It is still more unavoidable that the remainder of the continent should ultimately be ours."[38] Spain, however, was clear that the territory of Texas, from the Sabine River to the south, was not negotiable despite diplomacy and an offer of cash. Neither Spain nor Mexico would sell this land to the United States. By retaining Texas, Spain was guaranteed a borderlands area that was to continue to serve as a defensive territory against the North Americans. The Mexican government thought likewise.

The Adams-Onís Treaty was really a brightly colored feather in the expansionist cap of Secretary of State Adams. He had obtained for the United States both Floridas, complete control of the Mississippi, and direct access to the Pacific Ocean via the Oregon territory. Despite what seemed like a string of successes, many of the expansionists throughout the nation were not happy. In Congress, Representative Trimble raised an impassioned protest saying, "The great Engineer of the Universe has fixed the natural limits of our country, and man cannot change them; that at least is above the treaty-making power. To that boundary we shall go; 'peaceably if we can, forcibly if we must.'"[39] For Trimble and others it was the southern Río Grande where the "great Engineer of the Universe" had fixed the true boundaries of the southwestern United States.

For these expansionists, both in government and in the general population, the treaty of 1819 was seen as acquiescing to Spain. It meant losing land that had been "destined" to be part of the United States and was therefore interpreted as a tremendous loss. The Oregon territory seemed too distant and its true worth was not thoroughly understood at the time. It was much easier to perceive that Texas was the valuable territory that should not have been given up to Spain and that should have been part of the treaty negotiations. The reasons for the great North American interest in Texas varied.

For the southerners, eager for new land for their cotton business, the "loss" of Texas seemed like "a betrayal of the nation, a tearing apart of the valley of the Mississippi, an exchange of inner-valley unity for a slice of outer space [the Oregon territory]."[40] The discontent of some of these southerners translated into military action when James Long invaded Texas in 1819. His expedition left from Natchez, which had become "the rising new Southern center of the cotton kingdom."[41] Long declared Texas an independent republic, a claim that was quickly done away with when Spanish troops pushed him back into Louisiana that same year.[42] So while the treaty of Adams-Onís served to stoke the fires of the expansionist ideologies of the early nineteenth century, it also sowed the seeds of discontent regarding the Texas borderlands. This discontent simmered quietly into the late 1820s and 1830s until its mighty explosion in the 1840s.

Texas as Borderlands

The U.S. historian Herbert Eugene Bolton was the first to identify the geographical zone north of the Río Grande, which was the outer limits of Nueva España, as a "borderlands." For Bolton, "borderland zones are vital not only in the determination of international relations, but also in the development of culture."[43] Bolton believed that despite the fact that this borderlands region was Spain's outpost, meaning the northern fringes of its empire, it should not be dismissed as a territory that was unimportant to Spain nor one it had not colonized. What has happened is that in the history of these borderlands the dominant story does not give voice to the people who inhabited these lands before the arrival of the first Euro-American settlers. Their culture, language, religion, their very existence is either dismissed or relegated to a very unimportant historical footnote. However, Bolton was clear that this viewpoint was both erroneous and incomplete. It is important to understand the borderlands territories as "a social environment and not simply a physical or geographical environment"[44] that was created by what Bolton has identified as three important socializing forces. Spain systematically created this "social environment" by using the missionary to establish *misiones*, the soldier to establish *presidios,* and *colonos* (or *pobladores*) to establish civilian settlements. Spain's presence in North America extended east to the Carolinas, southeast to las Floridas and the Caribbean. To the north and west, Spain had left her mark in Colorado, in Nuevo México, in Nevada, and then California. But more important, Spain was able to create a web of social interactions and social institutions in the borderlands that were nonstatic and that shaped borderlands culture. So while it may have been true that Spain moved into these territories primarily to create a geographical defensive zone, this did not mean that the borderlands were less Spanish.

On its northernmost border Spain suffered the onslaughts of the French, Dutch, English, and Russians, not all at once, but in successive clashes;[45] eventually her most intense clashes took place north of the Río Grande and north of the Gulf of Mexico. Spain proved an aggressive opponent who continued to fashion a Spanish empire in North America in the face of its adversaries. Perhaps this is what both the U.S. government and the Euro-American settlers who moved into these Spanish borderlands did not fully comprehend or perhaps dismissed as irrelevant. Traditionally, historians of the Texas borderlands have primarily focused on military and diplomatic events, ignoring the dynamics of communities, language, religion, and race. Some have placed too much emphasis on Bolton's idea of the borderlands mainly serving as Spain's defensive outpost. Those who have ignored Bolton's statement about the importance of the borderlands to the development of culture have regarded this territory as a vast bare land which Spain vaguely remembered belonged to its empire. In this interpretation the Texas borderlands is relegated to a kind of "twilight zone" and perceived as a vast wilderness that was sparsely populated by a migratory people who left little historical record and had little cultural impact.[46]

Other histories have focused on Spain's military and political inability to control the expansionism of a superior United States. What is highlighted in this type of interpretation is the unavoidable progress

of a people much more ambitious and aggressive than those they encountered and the resulting westward movement of North Americans
as the national drama, or epic of the United States's great "errand into
the wilderness."[47] The subtext of this national epic must not go unread.
This reading of history presents Spain as an inferior opponent that had
become a weak corrupt monarchy that could not stand up to the democratic "ideals" of the new republic of the United States, which interpreted itself as the possessor of a great divine blessing. This historical
subtext makes clear that the principal focus of this interpretation is not
on military prowess.

Spain did effectively use its military strength to keep the filibusters
in check and it did not back down in any of her brief military encounters with the United States. What is fundamental here is the tacit acceptance of the key ideologies used by expansionists to further the
geopolitical agenda of the United States. Not only did the expansionists invoke the idea of geographical predestination but they were also
aided by the justificatory doctrine of the "destined use of the soil."[48]
This ideology was first used to displace the original borderlands people
from their lands. It was an ideology useful to the sixteenth-century Spanish *conquista* and useful again for the eventual subjugation of all the
Americas by Europeans from England, France, and Portugal.

The first appearance of this ideology can be found in the papal do-
nations of 1493 when Pope Alexander VI "gave" the Americas to the
crown of Castile. It was used again by the seventeenth-century American Puritans. John Winthrop of Massachusetts states this idea plainly:

> That which lies common & hath never been replenished or subdued to
> any that will possess and improve it, for god hath given to the sonnes
> of men a double right to the earth, there is a naturall right & a Civil
> right . . . And for the Natives in New England they inclose noe land
> neither have any settled habitation nor any tame cattle to improve the
> land by, & soe have noe other but a naturall right to those countries soe
> as if wee leave them sufficient for their use wee may lawfully take the
> rest, there being more than enough for them & us.[49]

In the sixteenth-century Spanish *conquista* the ideology of destined use
of the land, an ideology also held by the newly emerging United States,
carried with it notions of superior versus inferior, civilized versus savage, advanced versus backward. The land was destined by Providence
to belong to those who could "tame" its wilderness, extract its treasures, and thereby "improve" the land. Such an ideology could do
nothing less than imperil the land tenure of the Native Americans and
of the Mexicans.

This interpretation also lends itself to the creation of a racial and cultural dichotomy, which separates the "pure" (and therefore superior) Anglo-Saxon race from the mixed-race (and therefore inferior) "mestizo" people.[50] The undertones of this interpretation are certainly racist, but there is yet another level of comparison, another area in which to signify difference—religion. The idea of the difference in race between the Euro-American settlers and the Mexicans, with its associations of superiority and inferiority, has a direct parallel in the notion of religious difference. In the Texas borderlands this religious difference played itself out as Protestantism versus Roman Catholicism and was often interpreted in Protestant missions reports as "the pure Gospel" versus "popery" or "superstition."[51]

The tacit understanding is that God has willed the establishment of a new democratic and truly Christian (Protestant) nation on the North American continent. This was not possible with a backward, superstitious, Roman Catholic, "mestizo" population, who ultimately did not understand the ideal of democracy expressed through the creation of a republic such as the United States. This historical interpretation places Protestant Christianity as a strong and important collaborator with democracy with its republican form of government. The message is that the democracy of the United States is part of a grand design that enjoys both divine favor and protection.

This nationalist ideology embodies the belief that "one nation has a preeminent social worth, a distinctively lofty mission, and consequently unique rights in the application of moral principles."[52] The cause of liberty is now the "Daseinsberechtigung" of the people of North America—their national mission.[53] The religious myth undergirding this interpretation was that "Providence would not give up to military destruction a people striving for liberty."[54] It seems obvious in this type of worldview that Roman Catholic nations such as Spain and Mexico were "outside" the stage of divine providence, did not enjoy divine favor, and ultimately could not militarily defeat the United States. Some contemporary historians have argued that this ideology of Euro-American racial superiority became more clearly prevalent and jarring by the mid-nineteenth century and that it was truly evident during the Mexican American War (1840s). It is not difficult to find a historical record reflecting these nineteenth-century ideas of North Americans' innate racial strengths when compared to the people of color they encountered as they moved west. However, Latino historians posit that these same ideas were already part of the national U.S. discourse long before the mid-nineteenth century. These historians believe that the ideas of racial superiority and purity were part of the

Euro-Americans' worldview when they first entered Texas at the beginning of the nineteenth century.[55] It would also be correct to say that
these ideas were part-and-parcel of a national ethnocentric discourse
that can be traced to the seventeenth-century Puritan settlers.

When examining Texas and how this issue of race and divine elec-
tion played out, we can take as our first example the statement made
by the great *empresario* Stephen F. Austin. Austin sought to colonize
Texas with three hundred North American families through an official
Spanish land grant given to his father in 1820. Like the other North
American settlers, Austin carried his own understandings of race. He
wrote, "My object, the sole and only desire of my ambitions since I
first saw Texas, was to redeem it from the wilderness—to settle it with
an intelligent honorable and interprising [*sic*] people."[56] Austin is giving voice to a widely held assumption of his day and time: the more
energetic, ambitious, and capable Euro-American was no match for the
less capable, less worthy, and unassertive borderlands people, whether
they be Spaniard, mestizo Tejano, or Native American.

By uncritically preserving these interpretive lenses in our own national historical discourse, what has been lost is the importance of
the people who lived in and shaped the borderlands.[57] Lost is the
crucial examination and recognition of the vitality of the borderlands
itself as a place in which a new culture was shaped. By assuming that
the Texas borderlands was a forgotten land, or that the borderlands
was a place where the "superior" displaced the "inferior," the deeper
levels of meaning that belong to borderlands history are neglected
and the complexities of life in the Texas borderlands remain unexamined. What is overlooked is the fact that a rich life already
existed there when the U.S. settlers arrived. In the borderlands life
had to do with "land, water, labor, marriage, acculturation, and social interaction."[58] And ultimately the national history of the United
States continues to uncritically weave into its narrative the "wilderness" myth. We uncritically continue to hold onto a national self-
understanding which is necessarily embedded with the "isms" of nationalism, racism, protectionism, and individualism, which continue
to be part of the national mythology of the United States.

No matter what interpretive lens appeals to us, the historical fact is
that the frontier settlers of North America who moved westward in the
nineteenth century were emigrants entering foreign soil. In the crossing of each river in the province of Coahuila y Texas—the Sabine,
Trinity, and Nueces rivers—these Euro-American settlers were ille-
gally penetrating the Spanish empire of Nueva España.[59] Their arrival

into the Spanish province of Coahuila y Texas meant that these settlers were coming into contact with a people and a reality to which
"they" were the foreigners, the invaders, and the Other. The Texas
territory was not simply a barren wilderness extension of Louisiana.
No matter how unoccupied the expansionist North American politicians claimed these lands were, this territory was part of Nueva España.
This was a territory populated by a borderlands people whose worldview was not Euro-American. It is important to remember that by 1821,
a variety of forces had etched features in the Hispanic frontier of North
America which set it distinctly apart from its younger Anglo-American
counterpart.[60] That is why the history of colonial Texas under Spanish
rule is more than an irrelevant "prelude to the rest of the state's history."[61] To examine the Spanish Texas borderlands is to tell the history of a land that experienced constant and often harsh transition, a
land that held the memories of a people who conquered and were conquered. The Spanish Texas borderlands was a land with the racial and
cultural power to shape and reshape. What we must always keep in mind
is that in these border zones in which humans interact with one another
"such interactions contain so many variables, including the historical
moment, that the result is always unique."[62]

David Weber argues that the frontier experience affected the Mexican settlers differently than it did the Euro-American settlers. The main
reason for this was the culture each group brought with them to the
frontier. A part of this culture was that the Mexican-Tejanos tried to
assimilate the indigenous people of the borderlands rather than anni-
hilate them. Therefore, "the Hispanic frontier became a 'frontier of
inclusion' in contrast to the 'frontier of exclusion' created by the Anglo-
Americans."[63] This created a reality of life for the Mexican-Tejanos
that was not predicated on racial purity.

The fact that the frontier environment apparently limited natural
population growth meant that throughout the colonial period immigration was the primary means of demographic expansion. As a result,
immigration became a significant variable in the borderlands ethos.
Some scholars have even argued that this movement of people in "the
frontier environment removed race as a decisive determinant in socio-
economic advancement."[64] In the borderlands, Native People, Caucasians, and blacks intermarried and mixed into what were known as
castas. Each *casta* was assigned a certain status, and while the pure
Spaniards, or *españoles*, continued to hold the spot at the top of the
social ladder, racial purity "was certainly less important to economic
opportunity in Texas than in the heart of New Spain."[65]

In 1811, the liberal Spanish Cortes of Cadíz took the policy of acculturation to its logical conclusion by declaring the juridical equality of Indians and Spaniards throughout the empire.[66] The results of this legal document were mixed, yet the borderlands were forever altered. Beyond the passing of racial laws was the reality of the people of this territory who in their marriages were shaping a new future. With each passing generation the borderlands of Texas became home to a new and developing indigenous people called the mestizo Tejano, who uniquely and for the first time combined *la sangre española, india, y negra.*

These were the people the Euro-Americans encountered when they crossed into the Texas borderlands in the early nineteenth century. Stephen Austin's colony did not enter a "no man's land." They had crossed into a territory that was Spanish and then became Mexican, but was above all mestizo. They had crossed into Texas, a land whose inhabitants spoke Spanish and whose faith was Roman Catholic. These were a people shaped by a different reality and understanding of race, culture, language, and religion. These were a people whose interaction with their borderlands was different from that of the Euro-American settler.

> Partly because of the minority position as well as because of attitudes brought from the Old World, Hispanos tried to assimilate indigenous Americans rather than push them back or annihilate them. . . . The frontier and its indigenous peoples modified Hispanic society . . . so that it never became a carbon copy of society in central Mexico.[67]

And because of these fundamental differences, the worldview of the Tejano often clashed with the Euro-American worldview of the new foreign colonizers. The Tejanos Austin's colonizers encountered were a people who had inhabited these lands for generations, who had survived disease, hunger, and a harsh way of life, who had intermarried and had formed a new mestizo race as well as a borderlands culture. They were a people whose language and culture was connected to a Spanish past all the while being reshaped by their Tejano borderlands present.

Within this early nineteenth-century Texas reality a series of other cultural creations also had great impact on the Euro-American colonizers. These can be defined or understood as the other crucial variables in the borderlands equation. One such variable was the *rancho,* the land itself and its distribution and use. The Spanish crown, eager to have this territory settled, provided generous land grants to those who were willing to move into the borderlands of the northern provinces. Spanish authorities provided settlers with *solares* (town lots), *labores* (approximately 177 acres) for farming, and *caballerías* (about 100 acres), also for agricultural purposes.[68] While there were no *haciendas* in Texas, *ranchos* were prevalent. By the end of the eighteenth century there were forty-five *ranchos* in the province of Texas.[69]

The *rancho* was a borderlands institution that helped spread the Spanish culture. During the mid-eighteenth century, ranching began to flourish, primarily in Central Texas in the land between San Antonio and the Guadalupe rivers, considered the cradle of Texas ranching.[70] In addition to the creation of the market which produced meat, soap, hides, and candles, *rancho* culture also influenced the work done by the Euro-Americans who raised cattle on the eastern seaboard. The introduction of the Texas Longhorns not only meant that the Euro-Americans came into contact with a totally different breed of cattle, but also had to learn to ride the kind of horses and use the new techniques needed to work with these animals.

Another variable was the Texas *vaqueros*. Texas cattlemen drove herds southward below the Río Grande during the 1770s and 1780s.[71] The *vaqueros* created a cattle industry that brought with it "saddles, lariats, the roundup or *rodeo*, cattle drives, sports, branding practices, stockmen's associations, and price controls, in addition to the animals themselves . . . affecting both the society and the economy."[72] *Vaquero* culture also helped to create a jargon of Spanish origin that is still alive today. Words such as *mesquite, bronco, burro,* and *corral* have become loan words commonly used in English. Other words such as *lariat,* from *la reata, lasso* from *lazo, chaps* from *chaparejos, stampede* from *estampida,* or *cinch* from *cincha,* have been anglicized.

Another variable of Texas borderlands life was uncovered when historians established economic and social links between Coahuila y Texas and Louisiana. There is proof of the trade of cattle and horses for manufactured items and for tobacco.[73] This trade was mostly contraband and therefore illegal due to Spain's strict protectionist trade policies which limited the ports of entry. Nevertheless, tobacco, cotton, and textiles became a lucrative smugglers' trade for the Tejanos who moved these goods into Saltillo in Coahuila, most probably through Los Adaes and Nacogdoches into San Antonio de Béxar.[74] Not all trade was illegal, however; there was also legal trade of farm products and other goods in an annual fair held in Saltillo which was attended by settlers from Texas and Louisiana.[75] The list of good confiscated from a Don Marcos Vidal in 1776 gives an idea of what types of goods were being traded in these northern provinces of Texas, Coahuila, and Louisiana; it included "chintz from Holland, colored spun linen, flowered silk in various colors, German linen, embroidered black velvet, silk stockings, red hued satin . . . axes, pots, knives, scissors, coffee, muskets and other goods."[76]

The Texas borderlands people, who numbered about five thousand[77] by the end of the eighteenth century, had molded a culture unique to their time and place. Even as the Spanish crown attempted to regulate their every action, castas and mestizos still enjoyed relative autonomy. *"Obedezco pero no cumplo"* (I obey but do not comply)[78] was a common response to Spanish rule. These were a people who valued the physical prowess needed to endure a harsh life as well as the ability to meet adversity which was all necessary to survival in the borderlands. "Those living in Texas [were a people capable of] adapting a familiar ranching culture to the new land, enduring the rigors that accompanied life on the range, devising means of wringing a profit from contraband trade (primarily in Louisiana), and taking political stands expressing regional desires."[79] When on September 27, 1821, triumphant armies marched into Mexico City, marking the winning of Mexico's independence from Spain, "the people of Texas passed into the new age with their identity intact and confident of their ability to affiliate themselves with the political and economic structure before them."[80]

The Making of a National Identity

The Frontier Thesis

The Disciples of Christ, a denomination born in the westward moving "frontier" of the mid-nineteenth century United States, is described by Disciples historian Winfred E. Garrison as a "phenomenon of the frontier." Trying to examine the advances as well as the shortcomings of the Disciples of Christ, Garrison states the following: "Born on the frontier, [the Disciples of Christ] had only frontier materials out of which to develop the instruments of advancement, and this they did with laudable energy and notable success, but subject to the limitations imposed by their origin."[1]

What was this "frontier" and what were these "frontier materials" Garrison makes mention of? By what historical process were they created? What impact does this frontier history have upon the religious history of the United States as it intersects the history of the Disciples? The answer to these questions are found in the historical paradigm created by Frederick Jackson Turner when he developed his now famous "frontier thesis."[2]

Frederick Jackson Turner publicly presented his thesis at a meeting of the American Historical Association in Chicago on July 12, 1893, in a paper entitled, "The Significance of the Frontier in American History."[3] Turner's frontier thesis was to become well known to later generations of scholars and to stimulate much debate and controversy, yet it occasioned almost no reaction or comment on the evening it was read. Even the historians who received copies of the paper responded with little more than polite interest. For example, Dr. Francis Walker, President of the Massachusetts Institute of Technology, after receiving a copy of the paper wrote to Turner that he hoped to "find time in the future to read the paper."[4] Yet as Turner continued to develop the ideas of his paper, his frontier thesis not only became popularized, but also became "the most American of all explanations of the nation's distinctiveness."[5]

The paper read that night in Chicago was the result of earlier research done for two other important essays, one "The Significance of History" which appeared in 1891, and the other "Problems in American History," which appeared in 1892. It would seem then, that Turner's third paper, "The Significance of the Frontier in American History," was a logical progression in his interpretation of the frontier. In his first paper Turner wrote of the value of the continual study of the past. For Turner the study of the past had much more than just intellectual importance, it was also conducive to good citizenship. He writes in his first essay on history, "Historical study has for its end to let the community see itself in the light of the past, to give it new thoughts and feelings, new aspirations and energies."[6] Turner's next two essays continue to build on his idea that examining the past can help a community gain new insights and self-understanding. In his second paper he introduces two important concepts that are later more fully expressed in his seminal frontier thesis: the retreating frontier and the continuous rebirth of civilization that takes place on that frontier.

Despite the popularity and impact of Turner's frontier thesis, he was not the first to interpret the frontier as a decisive characteristic in this "nation's distinctiveness." Before Turner other North Americans, like Benjamin Franklin and Thomas Jefferson, as well as foreigners, like Alexis de Tocqueville and Lord Bryce, also saw the frontier and the movement westward to be an important force shaping the democracy of the newly emerging United States. In his writings at the close of the Civil War, the editor of the *Nation*, Edwin L. Godkin, also made the connection between the frontier and democracy. He wrote that "Democracy came from neither the [American] Revolution nor the decline of English nobility in America, but from the disruption of society as it moved Westward."[7]

And democracy was not the only characteristic being connected with the frontier process in the developing United States. Historian Francis Parkman believed that "contact with the wilderness endowed Europeans with a 'rugged independence.'"[8] George Bancroft had put forth similar ideas in his histories of the United States that focused on the period between 1600 and 1830. In these histories Bancroft highlighted and celebrated both the democratic ideals and characteristics of the people of the United States as shaped by the frontier. He wrote, "Nothing came from Europe but a free people. . . . the people alone broke away from European influence, and in the New World laid the foundations of our republic . . . The people alone were present in power. Like Moses, they had escaped from Egyptian bondage to the wilderness."[9]

Theodore Roosevelt described how the frontier had transformed the new U.S. citizen. He wrote in his 1889 book *The Winning of the West*, that "'[u]nder the hard conditions of life in the wilderness, those who migrated to the New World 'lost all remembrance of Europe' and became new men 'in dress, in customs, and in mode of life.'"[10] So we see that from very early on in the history of the United States the concept of frontier was being interpreted as a force that gave shape to two unique characteristics of North America. First, the frontier helped to shape the *public* persona, that is the political mind and institutions of the United States as exemplified in its democratic ideals. Secondly, it was also understood as an integral force in shaping the *individual* persona of the nation, that is the characteristics of its citizens, who are described as men[11] of "bone and muscle" who preserve their "republican principles pure and uncontaminated."[12]

The words of these and other writers show the many layers that make up the national historical narrative. Beyond the basic and fundamental truth that the United States had expanded across some three thousand miles at an accelerated rate throughout the early nineteenth century was the uniqueness of that expansioin, which these politicians, historians, and writers were explaining. There seemed to be a consensus that it was in that ever advancing frontier that "a new set of character traits emerged and somehow became the dominant ones in the national character as well."[13] Turner incorporated all these voices and interpretations into his frontier thesis. For Turner the frontier was more than a simply a geographical "fall line" or demarcation; instead, Turner understood the frontier as a geographical space in which a unique process took place. It was a process of growth and national development the likes of which Europe had never experienced; it occurred, not all at once, but in waves that moved across a vast geographical area. He wrote, "The existence of an area of free land, its continuous recession, and the advance of American settlement westward, explain American development."[14] While for historians today this statement may be interpreted as simplification and overstatement, Turner was defining in a new way both "the static and dynamic aspects of the frontier."[15] He wrote,

> American social development has been continually beginning over again on the frontier. This perennial rebirth, this fluidity of American life, this expansion westward with its new opportunities, its continuous touch with the simplicity of primitive society, furnish the forces dominating the American character.[16]

Turner begins his historical chronology of the various frontiers in the seventeenth century, when "the frontier was advanced up the Atlantic river courses."[17] He then moves to the eighteenth century when traders, who followed the Native People, were themselves followed by Scotch-Irish and Germans into Ohio, so that by 1790 the frontier had crossed the Alleghenies into Kentucky and Tennessee.[18] By the early nineteenth century fur traders were working along the Great Lakes and heading ever westward into the Rockies. Now aided by steam navigation and the opening of the Erie Canal, the move westward could not be halted. With the discovery of gold in California the frontier shifted and expanded so dramatically and so quickly that it "skipped the Great Plains and the Rocky Mountains,"[19] helped, of course, by the railroad and land grants.

Turner understood that each phase in the expansion of the frontier not only reduced the colonies' dependency upon England, but also marked the growing differences between the inhabitants of the frontier and the inhabitants of the eastern seaboard states. Turner explained the process this way:

> The West and the East began to get out of touch with each other. The settlements from the sea to the mountains kept connection with the rear and had a certain solidarity. But the over-mountain men grew more and more independent. . . . [So] we note that the frontier promoted the formation of a composite nationality for the American people. The coast was preponderantly English, but the later tides of continental immigration flowed across the free lands.[20]

As Turner traces this fluid westward moving pattern he describes how each wave of the frontier movement also continually pushed further and further away from the influence of the east coast. This was significant for Turner because the east coast was in many ways synonymous with England in that it was connected to what was old and not really *American*. Turner believed that it was in the frontier that the connection to both England and the east coast was altered and ultimately severed. We can say that the pioneer's connection to Europe had been reconfigured and transformed in and by the frontier. Turner wrote, "In the crucible of the frontier the immigrants were Americanized, liberated, and fused into a mixed race, English in neither nationality nor characteristics."[21]

Turner describes what he calls the "striking characteristics" of this new people who were shaped in the frontier. He writes:

> That coarseness and strength combined with acuteness and inquisitiveness; that practical, inventive turn of the mind, quick to find expedients; that masterful grasp of material things, lacking in the artistic but powerful to effect great ends; that restless, nervous energy; that dominant individualism, working for good and for evil, and withal that buoyancy and exuberance which comes from freedom—these are the traits of the frontier, or traits called out elsewhere because of the existence of the frontier.[22]

Turner celebrates this new people as distinct from the English. These are *Americans.* They were also the promoters of a new understanding of the individual as well as the begetters of new political ideals. And, for Turner, the powerful force at the heart of the creation of this new people and their new nation was the frontier: ". . . in spite of environment, and in spite of custom, each frontier did indeed furnish a new field of opportunity, a gate of escape from the bondage of the past; and freshness, and confidence, and scorn of older society, impatience of its restraints and its ideas, and indifference to its lessons, have accompanied the frontier."[23]

Key Ideologies and Their Importance for the Interpretation of Westward Expansion

The importance of Turner's frontier thesis and the reasons for its popular acceptance beyond scholarly circles have been a source of great debate for historians. Why has Turner's thesis worn so well? What has been its appeal? The historical literature that has debated these and other questions has been quite abundant[24] and, despite its critics, the frontier thesis still holds its own unique place in the history of the United States. Perhaps its success has much to do with the ideologies that Turner was putting forth. In keeping with his own understanding of the significance of history, Turner's frontier thesis seemed to accomplish what he had stated the study of history should do: it gave to a particular people, to a particular nation, "new thoughts and feelings, new aspirations and energies."

The ideologies incorporated into Turner's frontier thesis were not only meant to provide an historical interpretation of how the United

States came into being, but also to satisfy the need we all have for a "usable past." And the end of the 1890s was an age eager and willing to listen to Turner's historical interpretations. The end of the nineteenth century was a time when enough change had occurred in the life of the nation so that there was a romantic yearning for the return to a simpler and more livable past. By the 1890s the frontier, as understood to be where the triumph of the "common man" had taken place, was gone forever. It had been replaced by growing urban areas and a constantly increasing industrialism. Turner expressed his acknowledgement of the loss of the frontier in the last paragraph of his essay *The Significance of the Frontier in American History*. He made the following somber observation. "And now, four centuries from the discovery of America, at the end of a hundred years of life under the Constitution, the frontier has gone, and its going has closed the first period of American history."[25]

Bancroft had much earlier postulated that "the law of history was progress."[26] In the 1890s this progress was evidenced by a social evolution from simplicity to complexity, from the rural to the urban, from the agrarian to the industrial. This being the case, then the fact that the frontier was gone by the end of the nineteenth century was to be understood as part of that "law of history" and therefore as inevitable. Perhaps that is why Turner described its fading as the culmination of a "first period" of the nation's history.

For Turner this evolution in the frontier, when the rural-agrarian gave way to the urban-industrial, was important to the history of the United States. Turner wrote, "The United States lies like a huge page in the history of a society. Line by line as we read this continental page from West to East we find the record of social evolution."[27] Yet despite Turner's positive affirmation, that the frontier inevitably had to evolve and change as a byproduct of progress, it "did not disguise the frightening implication of Turner's essay that the achievement of civilization was offset by the loss of democracy."[28]

So we come upon Turner's quandary, which also seemed to be shared by the nation. What were the prospects of the nation's "ability to retain its frontier 'ideals' in the non-frontier twentieth century?"[29] Turner had understood that the end of the frontier also meant the end of a significant era in the history of the United States and that an abrupt transformation had again taken place. While it was a fact that not all "free" land in the West had been settled by 1890, when the frontier was supposedly closed, it was just as true that great changes had indeed altered the nation as a whole by the late 1890s. These could not be ignored.

The general optimism and hope of the antebellum years partially yielded toward the end of the[nineteenth] century to more sober assessments, doubts, and uncertainties. Many considered the defects of their society evidence that an earlier age's bland confidence in progress was un-founded. . . . Instead of the millennium, American civilization appeared to have brought confusion, corruption, and a debilitating overabun-dance. There existed, to be sure, a countercurrent in American thought of pride and hope, but the belief persisted that the United States, if not the entire Western world, had seen its greatest moments and was in an incipient state of decline.[30]

If we look to some of the literature of this time we will find that it bears witness to this overall pessimism and sense of loss.[31] For example, the 1898 publication of a book by Robert A. Woods, *The City Wilder-ness,* exposed Boston's slum conditions and the plight of the urban poor. Only a few years later Sinclair Lewis's book *The Jungle* was published, revealing the horrors of the Chicago stockyards right in the heart of "Mid-western America."

An interesting example of the fascination a romantic reinterpreta-tion of the frontier past held for many in the United States can be found in the (Boston) *Post.* The *Post* ran a series of immensely popular ar-ticles from August to October 1913 about a so-called modern primi-tive man. This modern primitive man, by the name of Joseph Knowles, had left civilization for the wilderness of the Maine woods in a publi-cized effort to return to a simpler, more natural lifestyle. When this primitive man finally emerged from the woods on October 4, 1913, he was greeted with a tremendous and unexpected wave of public fervor. Knowles's arrival in Boston on October 9, 1913, became a public event celebrated by thousands of people along the streets. The city had not had a hero like "the modern primitive man" in a generation.[32]

Roderick Nash in his book *Wilderness and the American Mind,*[33] which analyzes the nation's changing attitudes toward the wilderness, describes Boston's emotional response to the "modern primitive man" as an example of the "wilderness cult" that developed around the turn of the century. And he says that it was Turner who associated the wil-derness with "democracy and messianic idealism. . . . Turner recast [the role of wilderness] from that of an enemy which civilization had to conquer to a beneficent influence on men and institutions. His greatest service to wilderness consisted of linking it in the minds of his coun-trymen with sacred American virtues."[34]

In a time of rapid change and social upheaval Turner's frontier the-sis, with its layers of meaning, spoke to the nation in a language it understood and was familiar with. His writings about the frontier "contributed to a general sense of nostalgic regret over the disappearance of wilderness conditions."[35] Because Turner's thesis encompassed a series of auspicious ideologies and convictions they were embraced not only because they were interpreted as patriotic, but also because they provided an acceptable modern revision of what earlier voices had said America and Americans were all about.

Turner's ideologies, which were neither original nor exceptional, were also embraced because they painted a picture of the American and of America as unique creations. In the worldview Turner was advocating, the nation and its citizens were depicted as endowed with the kinds of qualities and abilities that not only were reminders of a glorious past, but also declared how the present and the future manifestly needed to be. It has even been argued that the frontier thesis "because of its mythical content appealed to deeply felt emotional needs of Turner's and subsequent generations."[36]

Turner's writings were an eloquent synthesis of the many ideas that had been part of the national discourse even before the generation of the Revolution of 1776, but there was more. Turner also wrote about the frontier as a scholar. This meant that he was able to provide a legitimizing scholarly framework that analyzed the frontier in a scientific and systematic manner. So Turner was able to speak and to capture the attention of academia, as well as the imagination of a broad spectrum of people beyond academia.

Even today, at the beginning of a millennium, we continue to see that the West, with all the implications of its geographical expansion, still captures the imagination of Americans. Although recent movies have depicted the Euro-American frontier movement from the perspective of the Native Americans or Mexicans, their impact has not been as visible nor as long-lasting as the larger-than-life Hollywood cowboy heroes of older movies. John Wayne, the ultimate cowboy, is still best remembered for his movie roles in the epic westerns that, even today, are still understood to depict what the United States believes it was and needs to continue to be.

What we have found in the frontier thesis is its power to transmit meaning through symbols. In talking about the frontier and its power to transform the European and to thereby create America, Turner is calling attention to a "symbolic frontier."[37] He is describing that other esoteric frontier that is full of symbolic, mythic, and aesthetic value. This "other" frontier captures the public imagination and continues to be the stuff of great folklore. The "symbolic frontier" is the place in which we find the "American Adam." It is where we accept the belief that America represented a second chance for Western civilization and that the pure and innocent Americans created a "redeemed" society in the New World freed of the constraints and corruptions of the Old.[38]

Surely the perception of "historian as mythmaker" is true of Turner and the symbolic meaning of his frontier thesis. In his analysis of the frontier Turner became the teller of the great story of "America's primal scene."[39] By fixing his story on the frontier itself he was continuing the seventeenth-century myth that North Americans built "their civilization out of nature itself."[40] Turner was giving modern voice and scholarly weight to the claim of the early settlers, and then to the frontier pioneers, that the impetus for the creation of their new society, as well as their new selves, came from the land itself.

What Turner was doing was writing a history that could be read on two levels. First, he writes as a son of the wilderness, someone who was born on the Wisconsin frontier in 1861 who is familiar with the terrain and the subject matter. As the writer of this story his between-the-lines message is the stuff of legends. But Turner also writes like the well-trained scholar he was. He had done some of his historical studies in Germany and then went on to complete his doctoral work at Johns Hopkins with the German-trained Herbert Baxter Adams. As the writer of this story, he not only formulated a thesis for understanding the formation of a nation, he was also able to train a generation of historians who continued to carry forth his ideas throughout the universities of the United States. His impact cannot be dismissed even if he is considered, by today's historians, simplistic and idealistic, someone who basically provided a "poetic mythologizing of American history."[41]

The Land and Democracy

A first and important concept found in Turner's frontier thesis, and one that has been discussed briefly, is that of "free land" or "wilderness." In Turner's thesis the land itself, the wilderness, the frontier, that vast expanse, was a decisive core element. It was in this wilderness or frontier that the United States was first shaped and then continually reshaped. Turner quotes Henry Adams's description of the United States in 1800 to give voice to his own appreciation for the land.

> See my cornfields rustling and waving in the summer breeze from ocean to ocean, so far that the sun itself is not high enough to mark where the distant mountains bound by golden seas. Look at this continent of mine, fairest of created worlds, as she lies turning up to the sun's never failing caress her broad and exuberant breasts, overflowing with milk for her hundred million children.[42]

This is no ordinary land. Instead it is a land that is the "fairest of created worlds" and so is itself a divine prize for a special people. In this national myth there is a "welding of the meaning of America and the continent."[43]

Turner also understood the frontier to be a place of "virgin" land that was there for the taking. He argues, "The most important thing about the American frontier is, that it lies at the hither edge of free land."[44] The land, virgin and free, was understood as a blank page on which North Americans could reinvent themselves. Now they were no longer English or European or even immigrants, they were Americans with all the promise that their new identity gave them. And an integral component of that identity was the love of liberty, the ideal of democracy. He writes,

> The wilderness masters the colonist. It finds him a European in dress, industries, tools, modes of travel, and thought. It takes him from the railroad car and puts him in the log cabin of the Cherokee and Iroquois and runs the Indian palisade around him. . . . He must accept the conditions which it furnishes, or perish. . . . Little by little he transforms the wilderness, but the outcome is not the old Europe. . . . The fact is, that here is a new product that is American. At first, the frontier was the Atlantic coast. It was the frontier of Europe in a very real sense. Moving westward, the frontier became more and more American.[45]

Yet the land was also a "wilderness" to be tamed and to be conquered. It was contact with this primitive environment that greatly shaped both the pioneer and the new society he was creating. Gone were the old and worn models of the parent civilization that were the legacy from Europe. There was a dialectical process at work in which the frontier, or wilderness, had to be faced, it had to be conquered, civilized, and in that process the pioneer and his emerging society were also transformed as something new came into being. These pioneers were now truly Americans precisely because they had faced and conquered the wilderness and because the wilderness also influenced and shaped them. For Turner there was great importance to this fluid movement that shaped both land and pioneer. However the greatest thing that was created in the frontier was American democracy. The frontier or wilderness forces created a democratic impulse which found expression in the new institutions and ideals of the frontier people. Turner wrote: "the fundamental traits of the man of the interior were due to the free lands of the West. These turned his attention to the purposes of civilization, and to the task of advancing his economic and social status in the new democracy which he was helping to create. . . . Energy, incessant activity, became the lot of this new American."[46]

So it was that Turner was able to link the wilderness with the formation of U.S. values that were interpreted as sacred to the nation. What is more sacred than democracy to the understanding that U.S. citizens have of themselves? And after their democracy, is not the land which they hold as theirs just as sacred? Land and democracy become inseparable elements in the self-conscious creation of this nation's identity. Turner was absolutely sure that "the most important effect of the frontier has been in the promotion of democracy."[47]

Yet the process was not a simple one because the land would not be easily conquered. In reality the pioneers faced natural obstacles and physical dangers; food shelter, and water were scarce, and they lacked organized leadership. The frontier was a harsh and lonely place to live but it was precisely because of its harshness that the pioneer was put to the test. The pioneers were forced to work with one another to deal with the natural conditions they faced. And the pioneer succeeded because he learned to live and to work alongside others as equals: "the free lands . . . promoted equality among the Western settlers, and reacted as a check on the aristocratic influences of the East."[48]

The harshness of wilderness life had a powerful equalizing influence. As they worked to build their societies up from scratch these people "were forced to be democratic by the pressure of their circumstances."[49] And so throughout the development of democracy it is the wilderness itself which remains the unmovable stage upon which the entire drama unfolds. The importance of the land as a mythical element to both the frontier thesis and to the national self-understanding of the United States needs to be recognized. In discovering its importance we find that "the crux is not who was there or who came there, but the 'there' itself, the primacy of the place over time and actors, who are all mutable while *it* remains permanent."[50] By holding the land as paramount, the frontier thesis can then claim that the wilderness is not only the determining place for the creation of a new democratic ideal, but it is also the place for the creation of a new people. However, there is one major problem with this national land myth which is either dismissed, minimized, or ignored. The lands of the western wilderness of the United States were never really "free" nor "virgin," nor unoccupied. What about the people already living in that frontier wilderness? What role did they play in Turner's thesis?

The Issues of Race and Manifest Destiny

In his description of the frontier Turner says, "the frontier is the outer edge of the wave—the meeting point between savagery and civilization."[51] Turner's use of the word "savage" is quite revealing. By calling the Native People,[52] who already inhabited the wilderness, "savage" he is describing how non-American they were and can thereby almost dismiss them as unimportant to the grand scheme of frontier history.

So we have come to a second fundamental concept in the frontier thesis, the people. But not just any people, in the frontier are found the new American people. Turner understood that these people, the Americans, were a unique product of the frontier and totally different from the native inhabitants they encountered.

> The West was another name for opportunity. Here were the mines to be seized, fertile valleys to be preempted, all the natural resources open to the shrewdest and the boldest. The United States is unique in the extent to which the individual has been given an open field, unchecked by restraints of an old social order. . . . The self-made man was the Western man's ideal, was the kind of man that all men might become. . . . Under such conditions leadership develops.[53]

The U.S. pioneer was described as free and self-reliant; he was individualistic in his outlook, not given to too much social and governmental restraint, could "seize" all the natural resources around him if he was shrewd and bold—which Turner knew he was. And so did Theodore Roosevelt. In a book he published in 1893 on Daniel Boone and Davey Crockett, Roosevelt described the type of person who was able to succeed in the frontier: he "must be sound of body and firm of mind, and must possess energy, resolution, manliness, self-reliance, and a capacity for self-help . . . [characteristics] without which no race can do its life work well.[54] While Turner and Roosevelt described this new person (specifically this new man), this American, in secular terms, there were other voices that had been expressing the same ideas about this new person but in religious language which placed upon the shoulders of these people an almost altruistic enterprise.

Almost two hundred years earlier, in 1702, the preacher Jonathan Higginson "described how God had intentionally opened the land for the Puritans so they could subdue the wilderness, plant colonies, erect towns, and settle churches."[55] What Higgins preached was the manifest destiny of the Puritans to bring their superior civilization to the Americas through colonies, towns, and churches. Initially it was thought that what the Puritans were creating was to benefit the Native People they encountered, however this idea was dismissed in the nineteenth century.

In his Second Inaugural Address Thomas Jefferson expressed his understanding of Americans and America: "I shall need, too, the favor of that Being in whose hands we are, who led our forefathers, as Israel of old, from their native land, and planted them in a country flowing with all the necessities and comforts of life; who covered our infancy with his providence, and our ripe years with his wisdom and power."[56] In 1850 Herman Melville describes Americans in his book *White-Jacket*; his words tell the story of a people who have a unique and lofty mission.

> And we Americans are the peculiar, chosen people—the Israel of our time; we bear the ark of the liberties of the world. . . . Long enough have we been skeptics with regard to ourselves, and doubted whether, indeed, the political Messiah had come. But he has come in *us*, if we would but give utterance to his promptings.[57]

Again we find an understanding that the destiny of the North Americans had a certain altruistic component to it. This time the North Americans are not only to benefit the Native People, but they are are also to benefit the world. It seemed that these North Americans visualized their nation as a Greater Britain; a nation that had its own particular *Volkgeist* destined by God for the benefit of all humanity.

The frontier Americans were seen as a new people favored by God with a destined mission, however the men, women, and children who already populated the wilderness were relegated to the status of "savage." It was a category that not only separated and distinguished the American from the non-American, but also assigned worth. The non-American was *savage*. And this "savage" was not dismissed by Turner but assigned an interesting and pragmatic role in the frontier thesis, that of "consolidating agent."

What Turner meant by this was that since "the Indian was a common danger, demanding united action"[58] the threat the native inhabitants posed to the pioneers created a need for army posts and government regulation which facilitated and even encouraged cooperation in the frontier, thereby aiding the progress of settling the land. Turner also acknowledged that the "Indian trade pioneered the way for civilization,"[59] which meant that the Native People helped to open up the frontier to the Euro-American settler and inadvertently aided in their own destruction.

For Turner these native settlers were destined to pass away, to die out, to be supplanted by a more progressive, resilient, and civilized people. Their ultimate demise was to be expected as a natural part of the evolution of the "history of progress" that was being lived out in the frontier. Turner believed that this truth was evidenced by the fact that by the time the pioneers settled the wilderness,[60] "primitive Indian life had passed away"[61] due to the impact of the earlier traders.

As they moved westward, the traders quickly followed the Native People's trails, established trading posts near the settlements of the Native People, and introduced firearms to guarantee their own continued advance. "Thus," says Turner, "the disintegrating forces of civilization entered the wilderness."[62] The disappearance of these Native People, whether a result of governmental force or violent confrontation with the pioneers, was interpreted as merely a part of the evolutionary and unavoidable progress of this nation's history. After all they were not truly American. This rejection of the Native Americans, as well as of other colored races, by the North Americans was one that evolved from the sixteenth to nineteenth centuries, becoming more virulent with each passing decade. As Reginald Horsman writes, in the movement westward between 1815 and 1850 the Native Americans "were rejected by white society" and "Indian Removal [legislation] represented a major victory for ideas which, though long latent in American society, became fully explicit only after 1830."[63]

It was at the time of the passage of the Indian Removal Bill of 1830 that political power was used to begin forcibly removing of the Native Americans from their lands in a show of "ruthless racial confidence."[64] Gone forever was the early idea that colored races could be made to come "within the fold of civilization."[65] And so, in what appears to be a progression of racist thought, during the mid-1800s a scientific attack was launched to show the inferiority of the Native American people. Examined from this perspective, it is not hard to understand why Turner would depict the Native People of the western frontier as an insignificant people, whom he relegated to the margins in his history of the United States.

Race is a basic force of the history that takes place in the margins. Race is also linked to the nation's self-identity and to the negative aspects of its own becoming. Yet this negative force is not acknowledged in the mythic understanding this nation has of its frontier and of its self. Turner barely gives race a fleeting look but, interestingly enough, he couples it with a second negative force, manifest destiny. Notice his description of the advancement of "civilized" people across the frontier.

> Western man believed in the manifest destiny of his country. On his border, and checking his advance, were the Indian, the Spaniard, and the Englishman. . . . Militant qualities were favored by the annual expansion of the settled areas in the face of the hostile Indians. . . . The West caught the vision of the nation's continental destiny.[66]

And so Turner incorporates the idea of "manifest destiny" not as a negative but as a natural component of the frontier person and the nation that was being created. As a historian shaped by his day and age, Turner reflected the national perception that there was something "special" and "blessed" about being North American. Yet the realization that being a favored people meant that others were disfavored was not included in the national discourse.

To talk about the advancement of the western frontier of the United States from today's vantage point means one must talk about race and manifest destiny. Because to talk about the western frontier as a prominent part of this nation's history means that the people who were kept out of the national covenant must now be included in that discourse. Their position at the margins of history must be acknowledged and then examined so that we can better learn about ourselves today. And what we quickly discover is that race and manifest destiny were two of the most crucial forces to shape the frontier and the nation.

It is a fact, unacknowledged by Turner, that when the pioneers packed their wagons and horses to go west they also carried with them the ideas and the values of the European world they were moving away from. Some of these ideas and values may have been abandoned along the way, but not all. Many simply remained, while others were reshaped or reworked so as to accommodate them to the new western frontier reality. One such important but often truculent idea that was part of the baggage of the frontier population was the nagging issue of race.

Once the white North American had convinced himself that he was culturally and intellectually superior to the nonwhite peoples he encountered, it was not hard for him to justify his aggression against them.[67] What exacerbated the contentious nature of the race issue on the frontier was the rapid expansion of the U.S. borders in the early decades of the nineteenth century. With each movement westward came a new opportunity for the aggressive encounter between the pioneer and the native inhabitants of the land. Each encounter usually meant conflict. "Convinced of their invincibility, the agents of conquest—traders, soldiers, missionaries, farmers, stockmen, merchants, politicians, railroad builders, and adventurers—swept across the continent. It mattered little what was in their way, human or otherwise; if it did not move it would be pushed aside."[68] These frontier settlers were a people who understood that they had a "mission" and a "destiny' to fulfill. The perception that the Americans were a people with a destined, and even divine, mission was especially prevalent throughout the early nineteenth century.

"Manifest destiny" and "mission," which were particularly popular terms in the United States in the 1840s, were "concepts that the Jacksonian Democrats themselves had occasionally employed to sanction their policies."[69] The 1840s were a decade of much change in the geographic contours of the United States, especially under presidents John Tyler (1841–1845) and James Polk (1845–1849). During their presidencies

> almost eight million acres of land [were acquired] annexing Texas in 1845, negotiating for Oregon south of the forty-ninth parallel in 1846, conquering and then acquiring by treaty California and New Mexico in 1848, and assuming jurisdiction over millions of acres of land in the Great Lakes region ceded by Native Americans who moved westward to the Great Plains. Never before had the nation obtained so much territory so quickly. In fewer than a thousand days, Tyler, Polk and their supporters pushed the boundaries of the United States to the Río Grande, the Pacific and the forty-ninth parallel. . . . In both its means and its ends, this expansion was unique in United States history.[70]

Fundamental to this remarkable expansion was the fact that these territories were already inhabited by non-European, non-Caucasian people. The Euro-American pioneers' response to their presence was not only to "push them aside" but also to conquer, dominate, and even exterminate them. This was done in the bloody wars fought with Native Americans, and also by continuous government policy and military supervision.

The Native Americans were removed through "encouraged migration and settlement, subsidized transportation,"[71] and extreme force. But not only were the Native Americans forced to give up their land and their entire way of life, they were exterminated in order to clear the land. These drastic actions were accompanied by a new understanding of non-white people that was rapidly developing in the nineteenth century and that incorporated social theory, science, and theology.

The first "sacred" concept that was reinterpreted in relation to race was that of the land or wilderness.

> The expansionists relied on other self-serving beliefs to explain and justify territorial acquisitions. They perpetuated the convenient myth of a vacant continent, invoking the image of North America as an uninhabited, howling, wilderness that the new, chosen people had transformed from savagery to civilization during their predestined march to the Pacific.[72]

What is implicitly being said here is that the North Americans' use of the land was destined. By appealing to a "higher law," that was divinely given, when the Native Americans refused to peacefully cede their lands, all the correct ideologies were in place to justify the use of military power to remove them or eliminate them. The political leaders of the early 1800s understood that as God's chosen people, Americans were entitled to the land. The governor of Georgia explained how the treaties with the Native Americans could be done away with using words that relegated the legal issue to religious dogma:

> Treaties were expedients by which ignorant, intractable, and savage people were induced without bloodshed to yield up what civilized peoples had a right to possess by virtue of that command of the Creator delivered to man upon his formation—be fruitful, multiply, and replenish the earth, and subdue it.[73]

The second concept that was also reinterpreted was that of the "chosen people" who existed in tension with the "non-chosen." It must be noted that not everyone in government or in the United States at the time condoned how the Native Americans were being treated. For example, William H. Crawford, who had been secretary of war in the War of 1812, had expressed that "the government hoped to keep the Indians on the lands they possessed east of the Mississippi River, and that he wished to assimilate these Indians within American society."[74] He stirred great controversy and bitterness in the states eager to dispossess the Native Americans by eliminating all their claims to the land. The idea that nonwhite people could be assimilated into the American culture was not widely accepted, and many even doubted it could be possible. What developed instead in response to the idea of assimilation were social and scientific theories that supported the Euro-American claims to racial superiority and helped to explain why these nonwhite people could never be assimilated.

The most popular of these scientific works was published by Josiah C. Nott and George R. Gliddon in 1855 and called *Types of Mankind*. This book, which in a sixteen-year period went through ten editions, provided a theory of racial determinism at a crucial time in the history of North America.[75] Not only were these theories important to the expansionists dealing with nonwhite people in the western frontier, but they were also important to the slaveholders. Both slavery and expansionism were significant concerns for the United States at this time.

In addition to the tensions already being expressed came the racial concerns that were beginning to surface in the 1820s as Euro-American settlers began moving into the northern territories of Mexico into what is today called Texas. Surely the people of the United States in the nineteenth century were being challenged, as never before, by the possibility of a multiracial nation that would include red-skinned, black-skinned, and brown-skinned people. It seemed that "the authentication of white supremacy nonetheless coincided neatly with slavery and territorial expansionism. Manifest Destiny and racism fed on each other."[76]

The fact that the concept of manifest destiny was also interpreted in theological thought and language is of great importance to our analysis. An examination of the use of theology to support manifest destiny helps us to better understand how the ideas of God as ultimate justifier of a country's destiny was able to strongly influence the ideas of race held by that nation. As Forrest Wood, who, despite his biases, has said so well:

> If Americans were destined to occupy the continent, some *One* had to make that determination. The term "destiny" assumed—no, proclaimed— the presence of a supreme force, an original mover. Inherent in the belief of being chosen was a belief in the existence of a Chooser, be it God, providence, nature, fate, or some other mystical entity. Once that belief was recognized, the rest was just a matter of carrying out the divine mandate so that its consequences coincided with the national interest.[77]

Such an understanding of history and of the individual's place in that history, as the recipient of God's unique favor and God's choosing, is a powerful concept. Its implications are capable of producing much hatred, inequality, and violence, for they not only single out a specific race, the "chosen people," but also single out a specific god. The expansionist, the slaveholder, and the imperialist of the nineteenth century were clear: the Caucasian Euro-Americans were the chosen race and the god that had deemed it so was the God of Protestantism. Forrest Wood even makes the claim that "Americanism and Protestantism were synonymous."[78]

This may sound like hyperbole, and perhaps Wood does exaggerate, but the strong connections between religion and state merit careful consideration. This is especially true given the vast Protestant missionary enterprise that began in the late nineteenth century to the Caribbean, Mexico, and Central and Latin America. It would seem that an alliance had been made. The church could now act as the state's partner, both working in unison for the glory of God and the well-being of the nation.

Something else of interest to note is how the many racist themes of manifest destiny played themselves out in the control and domination of the land itself. Turner's wilderness stage, on which the national drama unfolded, was not altered, even if the drama became more racist, even if it became full of conflict, bloody and oppressive. This was so because inherent in the idea that the nation had been chosen by God and had received a manifest mission, is also the belief that God's creation—natural and human—is there for the benefit of that chosen nation. Such an understanding only heightens the feeling that the chosen are a superior race better endowed by God to dominate and control the land and to displace or destroy the inferior races already there.

Beginning with the Puritans and continuing among the frontier pioneers, North Americans deemed Native Americans inferior. The idea that the Native Americans could legitimately own the land they occupied was denied "on the grounds that the [native inhabitants] had failed to make adequate use of the land."[79] Turner seemed to share this national racist attitude and so was able to easily dismiss the rightful occupation of the frontier lands by the Native People, whom he too labeled "savage." In giving voice to this idea Turner simply synthesized the views and values of many others before him.

In the South these ideas about race and the inferiority of nonwhite people were used to support and justify slavery. The work of men like Nott and Gliddon was expanded upon by other southerners who sought to bolster the idea of a "scientific" proof for the inferior nature of the African slaves. In the 1830s, publications like the *Farmers Register*, published in Virginia, the *Southern Literary Messenger*, and the *Southern Agriculturist* from South Carolina, all carried articles that argued for the superiority of the Caucasian race.[80] By the mid-nineteenth century the discussion of the superiority of one race over another was not just of concern to the South.

[E]ven those New England journals which were most reluctant to accept the new ideas readily admitted that race had become a topic of general intellectual and popular interest. The *American Whig Review* commented in 1849 that "ethnology is the . . . Science of the age . . . In the nation at large theories of innate racial differences were somewhat slower to achieve overt acceptance than in the South, but in the 1840s the new ideas infiltrated every section of the country.[81]

The spread of these racist ideas was aided by, among other things, the great interest in phrenology, which became something of a fad during the 1840s. Using the "science" of phrenology, these so-called experts traveled throughout the country "carrying charts, casts of heads, and phrenological handbooks, prepared to read a head for a set fee."[82] Their popular lectures made these ideas on race common knowledge in mid-nineteenth-century United States. What was their conclusion on the race issue? They said: "Caucasians were for the most part capable of indefinite improvement, while other races were irredeemably limited by the deficiencies of their original cerebral organization."[83]

These phrenologists defended the idea of inherent racial differences and of the superiority of one race over the other. They found in the skulls and heads which they "read" the physical confirmation or proof that many others around the nation, for a variety of economic and political reasons, wanted to hear. And many heard what they wanted: "Whites were inventive, creative, powerful; blacks were docile and ignorant; [Native Americans] were savage and intractable."[84]

The verdict against the nonwhite races in the United States had been made by a group claiming scientific support for their conclusions, and the implications of this racial assessment were evident. It was now up to the Euro-American Caucasian to carry forth the nation's development, to fulfill the national manifest destiny. "Science" had demonstrated that it was whites whom God had blessed with a superior nature.

> By 1850 the natural inequality of races was a scientific fact which was published widely. One did not have to read obscure books to know that the Caucasians were innately superior, and that they were responsible for civilization in the *world*, or to know that the inferior races were destined to be overwhelmed or even to disappear.[85]

A hierarchy of the inferior races had been produced by the phrenologists. In this hierarchy it is interesting to note that the Native American was placed below or as inferior to the person of African descent. This being the case, then it is not difficult to understand how the removal of the Native Americans from their land was further facilitated.

> The scientific attack on the [Native American] as inferior and expendable, which burgeoned from 1830 to 1850, gave many Americans the authoritative backing they needed for long-assumed beliefs. Frontiersmen were as pleased to accept the scientific condemnation of the [Native Americans] as slave owners were to accept the scientific attacks on the blacks. The dominant scientific position by the 1840s was that the [Native Americans] were doomed because of their innate inferiority, that they were succumbing to a superior race, and that this was for the good of America and the world. The impotence of the federal government in the face of the massacres of California [Native Americans]in the 1850s has to be viewed against the widespread intellectual and popular view that the replacement of an inferior race by a superior race was the fulfillment of the laws of science and nature.[86]

The idea of the Anglo-Saxon as a *racial category* was gaining more and more momentum as the nineteenth century progressed. Anglo-Saxon meant Caucasian, and it was also understood to mean innately superior to the other nonwhite people living in the United States. This became an important and useful racial category, especially given the types of racial encounters that were taking place in the country. In the South, slaveholders were seeking to justify and strengthen slavery, while in the West the pioneer sought to own and control the Native American lands. However in the Southwest something else was taking place. By the 1820s a group of Euro-American settlers was moving west and south of the frontier into the Mexican nation's northern state of Coahuila y Texas, and a new chapter to the unfolding drama of manifest destiny was about to be written.

> Waves of Anglo settlers first entered Texas when the Mexican government in 1821 granted colonization rights in the province to a Missouri entrepreneur named Moses Austin. Hundreds more followed thereafter, coming to Mexican Texas under the aegis of Moses' son Stephen, and other empresarios. Most were not radically different from the pre-nineteenth century pioneers. Like them, they entertained a strong belief in themselves and the superiority of their way of life.[87]

The pioneers moving into the northern territories of Mexico carried with them the same sense of destiny, mission, and superiority that the Puritans had possessed. For the Euro-American pioneers who entered Mexican Texas the vision was the same: tame the wilderness, introduce civilization, and with it, establish democracy. As a result of this process, Mexican Texas would begin to look like and sound like a part of the Anglo-Saxon United States.

Tejano historian Arnoldo De León emphasizes that the preconceptions the Euro-American settlers brought to Texas were not based on their dealings with the Mexican-Texans. De León argues that the Euro-Americans who migrated to Texas had little "contact with Tejanos up to 1836, [because] most of the Mexican population was concentrated in San Antonio and La Bahía areas, quite a distance from the Anglo colonies."[88] Nevertheless, the Euro-American settlers came to the Mexican territories with preconceived racial ideas that were part of the on-going racial discourse of the United States. Combining a "xenophobia against Catholics and Spaniards [and] racial prejudice against Indians and blacks"[89] the Anglo settlers were predisposed not to accept as equals the Mexicans that lived in Texas. These racial ideas were clearly verbalized during this early period of colonization. "The vigor of the descendants of the sturdy north will never mix with the phlegm of the indolent Mexicans," Sam Houston (the future hero of the war for independence) argued in January 1835 in an address to the citizens of Texas, "no matter how long we may live among them."[90]

At the heart of this rejection of the Mexican Texan was the perception that they were similar in their inferiority to the other nonwhite

Native Americans and African slaves. However in reality the Mexican Texans were not truly African and they were not truly Native American. As a result of the mixture of their race, their *mestizaje*, they were perceived by the Euro-American settler as an even more inferior people. An example of this type of thinking is found in a letter written to the *New Orleans Bee* in 1834, which described the Mexicans as the most "degraded and vile; the unfortunate race of Spaniard, Indian, African, is so blended that the worst qualities of each predominate."[91]

The Mexican appeared to the North American settler to be a racial puzzle. The prevalent assumption was that such an amalgamation of races must produce a people inferior to those of a pure racial stock, since North Americans' first encounter with mixed-race people did not occur in Texas. The incorporation of Louisiana was as fraught with racial anxiety as was the purchase of Florida. There was a great tension between the powerful expansionist aims of the early nineteenth century Euro-Americans and the reality of what to "do" with the lands acquired that were populated by nonwhite people. The consensus was that "continental lands occupied by inferior peoples would first have to be fumigated by American pioneers, who would ultimately Americanize the continent."[92]

And this is exactly what Stephen Austin, Sam Houston, and the numerous other North American settlers that moved into Mexican Texas did. They were "civilizing agents." Even though they were crossing into foreign soil, they continued to believe it was their manifest destiny to dominate an entire continent. And so,

> In the 1830s and 1840s, when it became obvious that American and Mexican interests were incompatible and that the Mexicans would suffer, innate weaknesses were found in the Mexicans. Americans, it was argued, were not to be blamed for forcibly taking the northern provinces of Mexico, for Mexicans, like Indians, were unable to make proper use of the land. The Mexicans failed because they were a mixed, inferior race with considerable Indian and some black blood. The world would benefit if a superior race shaped the future of the Southwest.[93]

Turner's frontier thesis, while failing to explore the idea of race and manifest destiny, did capture an important reality in the creation of the United States in his description of the settling of the western frontier. The personal and the national identity came together in the very earth, in the settling, in the colonizing of that vast expanse of land leading to the Pacific. To understand America one must look beyond abstract ideas and understand that America was born of a physical fact. The land itself provided the stage for creating the American. This American then created a nation and, even though the essence of America as a nation was the very physicality of the continent, its citizens were identified by their race, which confirmed their destined role to Americanize the continent.

That is why "frontier" became an archetypal word in the eighteenth- and nineteenth-century United States. It spoke of the universal reality for a people believed to be chosen by God to complete a manifest destiny in a "new" land. The "frontier" promised newness of life as that life was given shape by the forces found in the land itself. Yet the very inability to share the land with people of other races was a defect inherent in the American creation that was not acknowledged. The issue of race, like the other ideas found in America, was tied to the land and to who would control the land and its borders.

However, race, as interpreted through the distorted lens of Manifest Destiny, proved to be a great encumbrance. No one could anticipate that in the latter half of the nineteenth century it would cause the nation tremendous pain and loss. Nevertheless, in the early eighteenth century no clouds could be seen on the horizon and America continued to evolve. Ever moving westward also meant moving into the future, a future where it was not imagined that the horizon would ever be clouded by the tensions and conflicts of race. And when all that conflictive racial ideology exploded in a civil war, the land also became the recipient of the blood of Americans.

3

The Making of a Frontier Church

The Christian Church (Disciples of Christ)

What is today the denominational body known as the Christian Church (Disciples of Christ)[1] had its beginnings in the first decade of the nineteenth century in southwestern Pennsylvania. The Disciples were born in the frontier of the developing nation, and, as George Beazley argues, "cannot be understood apart from their [North] American environment"[2] and its accompanying ethos. A consideration of the development of this denomination within its particular environment enables us to then turn to an examination of the relationship of the Disciples to those among whom they lived and worked. In the midst of an expanding frontier, in the process of developing a national identity, and in the reworking of European concepts to fit the North American reality, can be found some of the forces that shaped the Disciples of Christ and gave it its strong frontier appeal.

The early Disciples are a tapestry of Presbyterian and Baptist threads, interwoven with the threads of Lockean philosophy and Enlightenment concepts, adorned by the scriptural threads that depict the church as one body, all gathered in a basic weave pattern whose primary colors portrayed a church restored to its New Testament origins. The beginnings of the Disciples can be traced to the year 1809, when Thomas Campbell (1763–1854), an Irish Presbyterian minister who had migrated to the United States two years earlier, wrote and published what is known as the *Declaration and Address*. This is the Disciples' statement of principles and is the second oldest important document in the history of the Disciples.[3]

Campbell had been suspended in 1809 by the Chartiers Presbytery and the Associate Synod of North America because he had invited worshipers from other branches of the Presbyterian church to share in the Lord's Supper. So, in writing this early document Thomas Campbell sought to deal with two key concerns that had been inadvertently reflected in the disciplinary action the Presbytery took against him: the connected issues of Christian unity and the restoration of a New Testament Christianity that had no need for creeds. These issues were not new to Thomas Campbell, who had already begun to address the problems of a divided church while still in Ireland.

In his *Declaration and Address* Thomas Campbell gave voice to the beliefs and principles of a newly emerging body called the Christian Association of Washington, Pennsylvania. He set down in propositional form a set of principles for a new society within the church that he and his neighbors formed. In these principles was his prescription for attaining Christian unity.[4] The underlying axiom was that Christians ought to be united by a common faith and an encompassing love so that there was no need for complicated and divisive creeds. Campbell wrote, "The church is essentially, intentionally and constitutionally one."[5] The Christian Association of Washington, Pennsylvania, gathered men and women from different denominations, not to create a new church body, but to work toward the restoration of the Church which Campbell believed had been "rent into warring factions filled with bitter strife because men had demanded that others accept their opinions and inferences as the very truth of God."[6]

In 1809 Thomas Campbell was joined by his son Alexander (1788–1866), who had traveled from Ireland with the rest of the Campbell family that same year. Alexander Campbell has been described as a man who possessed a powerful logical mind with "a rootage in the philosophy of John Locke, and a thorough knowledge of the Scriptures in their original tongue."[7] Alexander Campbell was also a man taken by the biblical call to unity, and he used his learning to formulate a systematic ecclesiology for the newly emerging association. Campbell sought to shape a community that would reflect his beliefs about the ministry and the Church. For example, he favored the use of the name "Disciples of Christ" for the association; he believed ministers should serve without salaries, he advocated organized cooperation among congregations; and he considered immersion the only scriptural mode of baptism, while granting that there were unimmersed Christians.[8]

About a year after the Christian Association had been formed, Thomas Campbell sought to reunite with the Presbyterian church. We see in Campbell's petition to the Presbyterians an effort to avoid forming a new denomination, a move to avert total independence from the Presbyterians, and an effort to make some attempt at reconciliation and unity. Campbell did not want to be "forced into the position of the leader of a separative sect pleading for union,"[9] but he had been encouraged by friends that his petition would be favorably received. Thomas Campbell appeared before the synod of Pittsburgh at Washington, Pennsylvania, in October 1810. He was granted a hearing in which he was questioned about the work of the Washington Association, but the synod was not positively moved. The synod's decision was that "movements like the Christian Association 'were destructive to the whole interest of religion by promoting divisions instead of union, by degrading ministerial character, by providing free admission to any errors of doctrine, and to any corruptions of discipline,' and it 'refused to accept the applicant for the above and many other important reasons.'"[10]

When Thomas Campbell asked the synod what were the "other reasons" for their refusal he was told:

> For expressing his belief that there were some opinions taught in our Confession of Faith which are not founded in the Bible, and avoiding to designate them; for declaring that the administration of baptism to infants is not authorized by scriptural precept or example and is a matter of indifference, yet administering that ordinance; for encouraging and countenancing his son to preach the gospel without any regular authority; for opposing creeds and confessions as injurious to the interests of religion.[11]

A public response to the synod's accusations was made not by Thomas but by his son, Alexander Campbell, at the semi-annual meeting of the Christian Association on November 1, 1810. Yet despite Alexander's energetic support and advocacy for the association the group was in a very ambiguous position. The association was not a church, the members of the association were not in good standing with their former churches, and any attempts to reestablish these connections were not going to be well received by the denominational bodies, as was made clear in Thomas Campbell's appearance before the synod.

On May 4, 1811, the association voted to reorganize as a church. They had now declared their final independence from all formal denominational bodies and elected for their leader Thomas Campbell as elder along with four deacons. In a bold move they also licensed Alexander Campbell to preach. On June 16, 1811, the group met at their newly erected church building at Brush Run, not far from where they had been worshipping. On January 1, 1812, the association ordained Alexander Campbell. Disciples historian W. E. Garrison interprets this act by the association as one which "further emphasized their claim to independence and their renunciation of all authority external to the local congregation."[12]

Earlier hopes of union with the Presbyterians were abandoned at this point. It was made even clearer that the association was headed towards irreversible independence by its position on baptism. Despite the fact that Thomas Campbell had replied to the Presbyterian synod in October of 1810 that "infant baptism is not expressly enjoined by Christ, hence . . . [w]e do not condemn it, but view it as Paul did circumcision in the case of Timothy,"[13] by 1812 everything had changed for the Campbells. In March of that year, Alexander Campbell, who had already immersed himself in the original language text of the New Testament to further examine the issue of infant baptism, welcomed the birth of his first child. A decision about baptizing the infant had to be made. His conclusion was that "those sprinkled in infancy had not been baptized at all."[14]

On June 12, 1812, Thomas Campbell, his son Alexander, and their wives were all baptized by immersion by a Baptist preacher in Buffalo Creek. They were also joined by three members from the Brush Run church that day. Thirteen others requested immersion at the next meeting; those who did not left the group. It was this step which brought the Brush Run group into relations with the Baptists and completed their total split from the Presbyterians. In the autumn of 1813, after prolonged discussion, the Brush Run church made application for admission to the Redstone Baptist Association.[15] It seems that the Brush Run congregation had taken another step in its tenuous process of self-definition.

It is interesting to note the forces at work in the shaping of this newly forming group. When Thomas Campbell appeared before the Presbyterian synod in 1810 he was still willing to "forbear" infant baptism, and the group had not really defined what they were, whether congregation, denomination, or dissident movement. But as the Presbyterians closed the doors on any possible participation or reuniting, Campbell and his followers began to move towards a clearer self-definition of their identity and theology. Their first definitive position was on baptism: baptism by immersion is the only scripturally sound form of baptism. They also continued to see themselves as a group outside the established church whose ultimate goal was to further the task of restoring the church to its New Testament origins. Because of their desire to return to a New Testament ideal, the congregation became the central unit above and beyond synods and presbyteries, which were not biblically sanctioned.

The Disciples now moved toward a possible union with the Baptists. The decision to join the Redstone Baptist Association was fraught with problems from the onset, since not all Baptist ministers welcomed them with open arms. In a written statement, which is no longer extant, the Brush Run group expressed their protest against creeds. This is significant to note since the Redstone Association had formally adopted the Calvinistic Philadelphia Confession in 1742. The request of the Brush Run group was simple: to unite with this Baptist body "provided always that we should be allowed to teach and preach whatever we learned from the Holy Scriptures, regardless of human creed."[16] Again we see that the Brush Run group understood that their mission was to seek both unity and restoration. They did not want to be a separatist group. They were seeking communion with another church body, but they were also making clear their theological position and their ultimate goal as restorationists who were dependent only upon Scripture.

The factors the two groups agreed upon were simple baptism and the organization of the local church. But as a union was being worked out with the Baptists, the Brush Run group continued to retain a theological distance on other issues, especially the celebration of an open communion (Lord's Supper). This showed that they did not really see themselves as Baptists, just as they were not really Presbyterians. They understood that their most important role was to be a force for restoration. As Garrison writes, "Their sense of a special mission was undiminished."[17] For a period of seventeen years (1813–1830) there existed an uneasy union between Baptists and the Brush Run church.

However, the alliance with the Redstone Baptist Association proved both helpful and fruitful to the Brush Run reformers. It expanded their field of influence and helped to open the way for them to work among the Baptists in Ohio and Virginia, as well as other parts of Pennsylvania. Alexander Campbell began to preach among the Baptist churches, though he was critical of their ministers and their claim to a special ordained ministry. With each passing year he developed with greater clarity the central position of his reform group, the restoration ideal, which he shared with congregations in a publication initially called the *Christian Baptist.*

Campbell's work as editor of the *Christian Baptist,* which he published from 1823 to 1829, helped to propagate his restoration beliefs
but also made him a nuisance to the Baptist leadership. In this publication Campbell attacked "clerical pretensions and titles; [biblically]
unauthorized organizations . . . ; and the use of creeds and confessions
of faith."[18] Running through all of his critical thinking was the desire
for union in the church, beyond creeds and ministerial control, an ideal
that remained at the heart of what he and his father Thomas Campbell
pursued.

A few years after Alexander Campbell began his publication of the
Christian Baptist, he and his father were joined by Walter Scott (1796–
1861). Walter Scott had been born in Scotland, was educated at the
University of Edinburgh, and came to the United States in 1819. Scott
became an evangelist of the Mahoning Baptist Association in eastern
Ohio. This was one of the Baptist associations that had responded quite
favorably to Alexander Campbell's writings in the *Christian Baptist.*
The coming together of Thomas and Alexander Campbell with Walter
Scott "was perhaps the most decisive factor in producing a complete
separation between the Baptists and those who were presently to be
called Disciples."[19] While Thomas and Alexander Campbell sought
Christian unity and restoration, Walter Scott was involved in "analyz-
ing the Scriptures in an effort to find 'the gospel restored.'"[20]

What Scott meant by "the gospel restored" eventually developed into
the now well-known Disciples' "five-finger exercise." This exercise
was Scott's evangelistic tool to explain the steps needed for salvation.
Scott's formula can be summed up by saying: God demands (1) faith
(which is belief in Jesus as evidenced in the Scriptures), (2) confession, and (3) baptism (by immersion as an outward sign of the inner
event); God gives (4) the gift of the Holy Spirit, and (5) life eternal.
Nothing in history lodged more deeply in Disciples' thought and practice than that formula, repeated for generations by thousands of preachers.[21] What we find here is the coming together of clear ideals and goals:
"Thomas Campbell advocated union, Alexander Campbell proposed
the reconstitution of the church, and Walter Scott rediscovered the
New Testament way of individual salvation, which he called 'Gospel
Restored.'"[22]

Scott began preaching this evangelistic message with full force in
1827 when he was officially nominated evangelist for the association.
It is not surprising that he was so well received, since those areas in
Pennsylvania and Ohio were already familiar with Campbell's ideas.
The message was clear, rational, and authoritative. It was presented in
a common-sense manner that had great appeal. The result of Scott's

work as evangelist for the Mahoning Association during that first year was more than 1,000 additions to the churches. That was more members than the whole association had had at the beginning of the year.[23] By 1830 Scott presented a resolution to dissolve the Mahoning Association, since he was convinced that there was no scriptural authority for its existence. He and others persuaded Alexander Campbell to support their resolution. In August 1830 the reformers within the Mahoning Association, now being called "Disciples," dissolved their association and began their gradual separation from the Baptist body.

As might be expected, the Baptists did not permit the reformers to continue among them. There already were Baptist ministers who were suspicious and uneasy with what they called "Campbellism." They claimed, rightly, that it did not really represent Baptist thought. Some associations, like the Beaver Association of Pennsylvania, the Goshen Association in Ohio, and the Tate Creek Association in Kentucky, soon publicly denounced the Reformers as heretical, condemning Campbell's doctrines. From Tennessee came a plaintive wail in the words of a Mr. McConnico, who wrote in 1830: "O Lord, hear the cries and see the tears of the Baptists, for Alexander hath done them much harm. The Lord reward him according to his works!"[24] By the end of 1830 the separation of the Reformers from the Baptists was fairly complete.

In a quest parallel to that of Thomas and Alexander Campbell we find another Presbyterian minister, this one from Kentucky, named Barton W. Stone (1772–1844). Stone was born in Maryland, grew up in Virginia, and began to prepare in North Carolina for a career in law but was soon "caught up in the surge of religious revival under James McGready."[25] Stone was eventually licensed to preach by the Presbyterians in 1796, and he would consequently join the Campbells and Scott, sharing with them both a vision for unity, restoration, and a manifest evangelistic zeal.

In 1801 Stone helped initiate a great revival held in and around Cane Ridge, the site of the log cabin church where Stone served as minister. "There he saw Presbyterian, Methodist and Baptist ministers laboring together . . . [and he] never forgot this experience of unity."[26] Barton Stone began to seek the kind of unity he had witnessed at Cane Ridge and which he had seen was possible to realize in the Church. His was a catholic spirit that struggled with the rigid Calvinism of his time. In his search for unity, Stone also moved toward placing a greater emphasis on the Bible as the base on which to build Christian fellowship. As a result, by 1804 Stone assumed a position of defiance against organized religious bodies when he "rejected all creeds and all ecclesiastical authority."[27] Stone's initial progress toward the quest for Christian unity began in 1804 with his withdrawal from the Cumberland Presbytery with four other Presbyterian ministers, Richard McNemar, Robert Marshall, John Dunlavy, and John Thompson, who together formed the new Springfield Presbytery. However, convinced by both experience and Bible study that the New Testament revealed no authority for ecclesiastical organizations, the dissident pastors could find no support for the creation of their own new Springfield Presbytery. So the decision was made that same year to do away with the Presbytery. It was disbanded on June 28, 1804. Upon issuing their final resolution, the ministers stated that it was their desire "that this body die, be dissolved, and sink into union with the body of Christ at large."[28] They were now free to "taste the sweets of gospel liberty."[29]

This liberty, however, proved to be difficult to maintain. Within a short time, four of the five dissident ministers sought the fellowship of denominational affiliation. Only Stone remained faithful to his vision as he continued as an independent itinerant preacher in Kentucky, Ohio, and North Carolina. There he helped to organize so-called Christians, which were independent churches. In 1824 Barton Stone met Alexander Campbell and each was "impressed . . . with the similarity between their pleas for simple and evangelical Christianity."[30] However, despite their common ideal and quest, there were differences to be overcome.

The main point of disagreement between Campbell and Stone was the issue of baptism by immersion. Campbell believed it was necessary for church membership, while Stone refused to have it used as a test of fellowship. A second point of difference had to do with the fact that Disciples celebrated a weekly Lord's Supper, while the Christians did so less frequently. A third difference was Stone's familiarity with the frontier camp meeting and his validation of this type of religious experience. Although he readily condemned any excess of emotion, he also saw the positive side to revivalism. Campbell was not in favor of camp meetings and voiced his disapproval in the October 1843 issue of the *Millennial Harbinger*. His preference was for an evangelism capable of mixing emotion with reason. The fourth difference had to do with the name the group was to use, Barton's group preferred using the name "Christian," while Campbell held to "Disciples." All along both men claimed biblical precedents for such usage. Even though Thomas Campbell and Walter Scott supported Stone in the use of "Christian" for the name of their united group, Alexander refused to give in. Finally deciding that no one group had a monopoly on biblical precedent and wishing to move beyond trivial issues, both names were kept. This compromise, and Stone's yielding to Campbell on the baptism issue, helped both groups move towards union. However the road still proved rocky, as evidenced by the continued heated exchanges between Campbell and Stone in 1831.

Union was finally to become a reality as a result of a Christmas Day service held in Georgetown in 1831. This event, shared by two congregations, one Disciples and one Christian, marked the beginning of a four-day conference. Within a few weeks a second, larger, meeting was held in Lexington, Kentucky, and so it was that on January 1, 1832, the Campbell "Disciples" joined with Barton W. Stone and his "Christian" group from Kentucky. An estimated 12,000 Disciples and 10,000 Christians came together in those early years of the 1830s.[31] This union marked the beginning of a religious partnership which, despite its emphasis on unity and its rejection of human organizations, became a distinct religious body with its roots in the North American frontier.

Historical Realities

The years 1830 to 1860 were a time of continued growth, a time to consolidate gains, and a time to begin to shape an identity.[32] In addition to seeing a growth in membership, many able preachers were also added to the Disciples of Christ movement, which served as a further catalyst to the evangelism already taking place. Yet in the face of such immense growth, the Disciples numbered over 225,000 in the late 1800s,[33] the group lacked an initial organizational plan that would help to create the kind of connections and clarity of vision that were needed to bring the entire movement into a cohesive whole. The plea of the Reformers remained remarkably simple: union based upon the gospel of "faith, repentance, and baptism."[34] Alexander Campbell continued his familiar criticism of "clerical domination." This helped him maintain an environment that fostered a democratic understanding of leadership that assured continued lay participation.

In keeping with the doctrine of ministry that was not exclusive, congregations ordained qualified men as bishops or elders who presided at the Lord's Supper and provided pastoral care to the worshipping community. Others were also ordained as deacons to carry out diverse forms of service, while a third group, evangelists, carried out an itinerant ministry of preaching. The participation of these men, most of whom held secular occupations and were not theologically trained, was focused on preaching and bringing the gospel to the unsaved. The preaching of the Disciples made a successful appeal to a large class of people who were too unmystical to have the kind of ecstatic religious experience both Calvinistic Baptists and Arminian Methodists insisted upon as evidence of God's acceptance, and too honest to pretend to have it.[35]

Two tools were used in this early period of consolidation to create some sort of unity and promote cooperation among joining groups. One was the printed word; the second was preaching. To enhance communication among members of the rapidly expanding movement and to help shape an identity, Campbell published a periodical called the *Millennial Harbinger*. This periodical was originally published under the name the *Christian Baptist*, but Campbell stopped publishing it under that name in July 1830, stating that, "hating sects and sectarian names I resolved to prevent the name of Christian Baptists from being fixed upon us."[36] The *Millennial Harbinger* was published monthly from 1830 until 1870. It proved to be an influential instrument for the transmission of the Disciples' ideas that helped to nourish the restoration ideal, which continued to fuel the Reformers.

Preaching was also used to create a sense of unity, but it was preaching done in a particular setting, known as the camp meeting. These camp meetings were effective not only because they were familiar to the frontier population, but also because they brought large numbers of people from different geographical areas together in a designated location. In 1835 thirteen congregations met in Wheeling, Virginia, to discuss methods of cooperation and the sending out of evangelists. Similar meetings were held in 1833, 1834, and 1835 in Deavertown, Ohio, also to discuss methods of cooperation and a plan for evangelism. The need for this type of dialogue and planning was made plain in the coming together of congregations from different areas, yet this need was always examined in the light of biblical truths. A crucial question was raised: were such meetings to plan cooperative efforts supported by the Bible? Eventually in later years the Disciples would come into strong conflict over the creation of voluntary societies, but in this early period Disciples acknowledged the need for cooperation and the need to set up a mechanism to help achieve it. As a first step and in an affirming response to this basic need, the first national convention of Disciples congregations, representing one hundred congregations, was held in Cincinnati, Ohio on October 24–28, 1849.

The preaching tours of Disciples evangelists were also used to promote growth and the restoration ideal. Men like John Rigdon from Illinois, John O'Kane from Indiana, and Thomas McBride from Kentucky were sent out as evangelists for the Disciples to help organize new congregations.[37] Alexander Campbell's tours were aimed at building morale and creating awareness of the Disciples among frontier people. The focus of many of these sermons was on Christian unity and the need to return to the New Testament church ideal. The Disciples' strategy "seemed self-evident in a newly settled country without an established religion where most of the population was unchurched and scores of denominations, mostly imported from Europe, offered their conflicting and competing appeals." The ultimate goal was, as Thomas Campbell said, to "take up things just as the apostles left them."[38]

So the Disciples flourished on frontier soil. It is fairly easy to identify the factors that contributed to this early growth: (1) the use of the press and the gathering of folks in what became yearly assemblies; (2) the preaching tours of able evangelists; and, (3) the tides of migration westward, which they followed. However, despite the gains and the growth, there were moments of tension and conflict with other denominational groups that had much to do with how Disciples understood themselves.

For example, Alexander Campbell and the Reformers refused to call themselves a church. But they claimed a unique status. Their churches were Simon-pure "Churches of Christ." They were "Christians only," while all others were sects and sectarians.[39] They especially enjoyed the fact that they were called simply "Christians" with no obvious denominational ties. Simply put, the Disciples saw themselves as reformers involved in a restoration movement. The result of this was that they were viewed with suspicion by other Christians. Many in the other organized church bodies resented their assertive style of evangelism, especially when it was carried out among their own members.

The occasional skirmishes with Baptists, Methodists, and Presbyterians over "soul winning," and the Disciples' aggressive practice of evangelism, often became bitter. A letter written in 1832 by a Disciple in Kentucky "complains that Baptists, Methodists and Presbyterians had united against the Disciples, that it was impossible to get the use of their churches."[40] Yet not all churches proved unfriendly and some opened their doors in a spirit of unity. In any case, in spite of opposition, and with or without cooperation, the Disciples continued to go about their work of restoration.

Central to both the evangelism that the Disciples carried on and to their understanding of authority was that of the Bible. Like the earlier European reformers before them, the Campbells sought a road to true Christian unity. This was to be achieved by "the restoration of the essential features of primitive Christianity."[41] At the heart of this Christianity was the lordship of Jesus Christ. It was the revelation of God in the person of Jesus that was found in the Bible, and so the Bible was at the center of the life of the congregation and the Christian. Alexander

Campbell wrote, "we take the Bible, the whole Bible, and nothing but the Bible as the foundation of all Christian union and communion."[42]

By taking this key position in regard to the authority of the Bible, the Disciples were appealing to a source of authority that they believed was accessible to all and not under the control of academics or clergy. The laity could freely approach Scripture and find answers to their questions without any clerical mediator. This is not to say that Alexander Campbell advocated a simple literal position in regard to biblical interpretation. On the contrary, Campbell helped to create a tradition of hermeneutics based on his own biblical scholarship. As a practical theologian who sought to interpret his reality and his faith, Campbell "inculcated a set of rules for interpreting a passage of Scripture. . . . he further insisted that no point of doctrine be established on a single isolated text, but that all biblical passages bearing on a question be examined and considered in their relationship to one another."[43] Yet the Bible remained accessible to all Christians.

It was on this basis of the appeal to Scripture as sole authority for their restoration ideal that Campbell was able to also support his rejection of creeds which were seen as divisive. For Campbell the slogan was simple, "Bible names for Bible things." This type of thinking helped him to discard a theological vocabulary that used words such as Trinity and consubstantiation, not because Campbell did not believe in these concepts, but because he understood these words to be merely human "tools for conveying human opinion rather than biblical doctrine."[44] Campbell believed that when creeds used a language not found in the Bible, "they usurped a magisterial function that belonged to the Bible alone, and they served to divide the Christians whereas the Bible served to unite."[45]

The liberation that this type of thinking produced was quite appealing because it delivered them from divisive human theologies while it acknowledged the Enlightenment concept of the intellectual ability of humans. Alexander Campbell urged his followers to open their Bibles and "hearken to the voice of God, which is the voice of reason."[46] It was possible for a lay person to approach Scripture and to understand it without clerical interpretation or oversight. The appeal of such access to holy writ and such confidence in human ability did not go unnoticed in the frontier environment. In an address delivered in 1836 Alexander Campbell said, "Man by nature is, and of right ought to be a *thinking* being. Hence it is decreed that, as a matter of policy, of morality and of religion, he ought not only to think, but *to think for himself*."[47]

Independence of judgement as well as clarity and simplicity of thought were highly prized on this North American frontier and the

Disciples offered both. By holding to the phrase, "No Creed but Christ," the Disciples placed the lordship of Christ as central to the life and work of the church. This implied that this church body was to stand separate from the secular world around it and its institutions which were infested with corruption and sin. Again, the appeal of such thought in a frontier environment cannot escape us. The belief in a frontier in which there was the possibility of building a new society with new institutions "encouraged the belief that the church could also be transformed into what God intended for it to be."[48] This was the possibility that the Disciples reformers held out to the population of the frontier.

For Disciples today the possibility of restoration which the nineteenth century reformers believed in is often considered "primitive" and interpreted as "a misreading of history."[49] It was a principle, contemporary Disciples argue, that ignored human influences and errors that shaped that early Christian community while holding to the belief that New Testament Scripture contained an inerrant accounting of the apostolic church. Some even call this early restorationist position an "exercise in nostalgia."[50] In spite of what contemporary critics say, what must be kept in mind is that for the founders of the Disciples movement this ideal was also reinforced and in many ways supported by the early nineteenth century unfolding of the western frontier and the perceptions that explained and defined that same frontier.

The idea of restoration has a long history. To accomplish the return to a "primitive Christianity" is an ideal that has filled the hearts and captured the minds of many Protestant reformers throughout the last centuries, including those of the Campbells and Barton Stone. But for the Disciples the restoration ideal was taking shape in a particular historical place, with its particular influences. For example, it is worth noting that because of the geographical distances between these nineteenth-century leaders, it is doubtful that these men knew about one another, yet we find them sharing almost parallel concerns and simultaneous efforts. Given the unsophisticated and limited means of communication available in the mid-1800s, we must look for other forces at work that helped to promote this shared vision of restoration and Christian unity.

One important common influence on the thought of both Thomas and Alexander Campbell as well as Barton Stone, was the writings of John Locke. Alexander Campbell, who had read *Letters on Toleration* as a boy, called Locke "the Christian philosopher" and, as W. E. Garrison writes, much of his own thinking was cast in the model which Locke's theory of knowledge furnished."[51] In a debate with Robert Owen in 1829 Campbell gave high praises to Locke's essay, describing it as a force "that first burst the chains that held England and Europe fast bound under a religious and civil despotism."[52] In Locke's focus on rationalism we can better understand Alexander Campbell's deep suspicion of the emotionalism so prevalent in the camp meetings of his day, just as Locke's ideas about the individual surely contributed to the great importance the Campbells also placed on the claims of the individual, as well as on the freedom and value of the individual.

Another important Lockean concern that influenced the early Disciples leaders was his view of religious toleration. Locke held that differences of opinion were not a reason for controversy, persecution, or division. Here again we see Locke's influence reflected in the Campbells' willingness to steer clear of trivial issues that mattered little in the long run and their reluctance to adhere to any formal creed which might lead to further differences of opinion and disunity. Locke certainly can be defined as a major force in the shaping of early Disciples thought, but there were other forces also at work.

Alexander Campbell was also decisively influenced by what historians have come to call "left-wing Protestantism," the ideas and culture of religious groups "which insisted upon the separation of church and state and denied the latter any authority in matters of religion."[53] This type of thinking is exemplified by the sixteenth-century Anabaptists and Spiritual Reformers. The left-wing Protestants of the sixteenth century shared these four characteristics:

> the ethical note, or the ideal of a pure church; Christian primitivism, or the attempt to restore primitive Christianity on the basis of biblicism of either the Old or New Testament; a heightened sense of eschatology, which in some instances passed over into revolution but more often took the form of a passive and patient enduring of present evils while awaiting the coming millennium; and the radical separation of church and state.[54]

It is not difficult to find these four characteristics in the nineteenth-century theology Alexander Campbell was developing for the Disciples. He was not only a primitivist, he also saw the church as self-governing, autonomous, and separate from the state. While Campbell himself may not have admitted to any direct connection between his views and those of left-wing Protestantism or his Seceder background, and while he probably would have claimed that his primitivism was derived directly from the first-century church, the influences of both the left-wing Protestant sects and John Locke cannot be ignored.

Another factor that cannot be ignored is that Campbell habitually read in French.[55] His sympathy lay with the people of the French revo-

lution, particularly with their stance against the clergy and ecclesiastical structures. Like the French revolutionaries, Campbell wanted to
undermine "the basis of authority in established religion" and "was a
freethinker who opposed all authority and all tradition in organized
religion."[56] Again we must note the appeal that such a nonhierarchial
religious movement would have in the United States borderlands/fron-
tier of the early nineteenth century. While it should be noted that initially Campbell was involved in what seemed a blanket assault upon
the clergy and their corruption of Christianity, he began to move towards a more discriminating attack on specific issues in the 1830s and
beyond. For example, he was particularly concerned with Roman Catholicism, which he claimed was a source of corruption of Christianity because of the alliances it had created between priests and rulers
and because it produced a "creed-making ecclesiasticism which produced religious sectarianism."[57] Campbell said that, "if Christianity was
persecuted by its enemies, it was corrupted by its friends."[58]

We also find that the Campbells and Stone were in revolt against
the dry and mechanical Calvinism they had inherited. There was a
hunger for a more personal, individual encounter with God. Alexander
Campbell in particular was much influenced by a new theological current called "covenant theology," which originated in Holland in the
seventeenth century and was quite in vogue in the Seceder branch of
the Presbyterian church the Campbells came from. "Following the
principles of this theology, he came to emphasize the idea of a development in God's relations with man and the sharp distinction between
the three dispensations—especially between the Old Testament and the
New."[59]

In this theology, humans also have the ability to choose or to reject
the terms of God's covenant, a covenant which has changed over the
course of human history, from the first patriarchal covenant, to the
Mosaic (for Jews only), and finally to the Christian covenant. This
meant that the Christian must follow the New Testament when perti-
nent commands are given.[60] Because his theology was more Arminian
than that of the Baptists, Campbell was never really at home among
them. The Baptists themselves were also troubled by this type of thinking. During the period of union with the Baptists, Alexander Campbell's
covenant theology was viewed with suspicion and considered dangerous. While Campbell was able to influence some Baptist associations
to support his theological position on the issue of covenant theology,
on the whole his ideas were deemed not truly Baptist, and many Baptist doors were closed to his preaching.

Despite the controversy it engendered, the ideal persisted for these early Disciples: Unity was to come from the restoration of a New Testament simplicity to Christianity. This restoration ideal valued the worth of the individual, respected the authority of the local congregation, called for a nonhierarchical ministry, preached a simple and biblically focused message which called the sinner to repentance and also advocated immersion into the baptismal waters. The same restoration ideal made the Lord's Supper a celebration in which creeds were not important. The fellowship of the table became a gathering place for all Christians.

The Disciples had much in common with the frontier world of the nineteenth century. The frontier environment was one which also held the individual in high regard. It also valued human reason and fostered the ideal of reformed society. The frontier ethos was not concerned with hierarchy but championed the "common man." The Disciples and the frontier "understood" one another. Clark Gilpin, a Disciple historian who has written on the theme of "faith on the frontier," says that,

> the Disciples of Christ were the quintessential frontier religious group, revolting against "aristocratic" Calvinist theology in the name of a simple scriptural message that was available to all regardless of education and revolting against hierarchical church government in the name of a simplified and lay oriented polity that recognized the democratic self-reliance of the pioneer.[61]

The Disciples of Christ were, as described by Sydney Ahlstrom, "a popular, down-to-earth form of eighteenth century Christian rationalism, a movement all the more striking because it was successfully propagated in the ethos of revivalism and by an adaptation of its methods."[62]

From Restoration to Civil Religion

Of great importance to the ideal of restoration envisioned by the early Disciples was the idea of a coming millennium. One of the primary reasons Campbell relied on restored, primitive Christianity to inaugurate the millennium was because only the restored church, he thought, could produce the unity in both church and society that was requisite to the millennial age.[63] The simple gospel message, preached to all who would hear, Campbell believed, would be able to bring about the changes needed to initiate the ultimate religious and political order of society. Yet a shift in Campbell's position of 1823 to 1830 and his later position from the early 1830s to the 1850s can be traced from his writings.[64]

In this gradual shift we find Campbell moving from the position of a radical restorationist to that of a supporter of the civil religion of the new nation. This shift came through his acknowledgment of a common religion, to use Peter Berger's term a "sacred canopy," that seemed to be able to foster pluralism, while it secured liberty, promoted unity, and celebrated religion. It is important to note this steady but important shift in Campbell's thinking, because it helps to see the impact of the forces that were at work shaping the thought and culture of early to mid-nineteenth century North America. If Campbell did indeed begin to embrace the civil religion of the new republic, as Richard Hughes argues, then Campbell, like many other religious leaders in mid-nineteenth-century North America, was being affected by the ethos of a culture in a particular time and place. There took place, in this frontier environment, a melding of religious ideology and expectation with the "transcendent universal religion of the nation"[65] which gave ultimate credence to a way of life that is still today called the "American Way of Life."

In Campbell's publication, the *Millennial Harbinger*, there can be found evidence of his shift in thought. In the February 1830 issue, Campbell wrote an article in which he stated, "there is now a scheme of things presented, in what is called the *Ancient Gospel*, which is long enough, broad enough, strong enough for the whole superstructure called the Millennial Church—and . . . it will alone be the instrument of converting the whole human race, and of uniting all Christians upon one and the same foundation."[66] The continued primary goal for Campbell was unity through diversity, that is, a bringing together of people despite their diversity. Here again we see the Lockean influence. Locke's notion that in the heart of humans there was a God-given "law of nature" which was discernible by reason and adequate for both social and political relationships can be found in Campbell's vision. Humans are capable of this discernment, which makes it possible to envision the coming of a new age.

But in addition to the restorationist goal of unity, the idea that it was in God's plan that a new society also be created in the North American continent resonated deeply in the expanding borderlands of the nineteenth-century United States. Like the founders of the new republic whose great political influence was also John Locke, Alexander Campbell "worked within the framework of the same political philosophy which had found expression in the Declaration of Independence and the Bill of Rights."[67] We can say that Campbell shared a common discourse with the revolutionaries of 1776 and that he shared with the frontier people of the early nineteenth century a joyful enthusiasm for the new country. In a letter dated 1815 to his Uncle Archibald, in Newry, he had this to say about the United States: "I cannot speak too highly of the advantages that the people in this country enjoy in being delivered from a proud and lordly aristocracy . . . I would not exchange the honor and privilege of being an American citizen for the position of your king."[68]

Campbell would eventually show evidence of disillusionment with the republic's government in the early 1830s after his involvement with the Virginia Convention, where he experienced firsthand the force of vested political interests. He was also greatly moved by the failure of this same Convention to respond to the Nat Turner insurrection. In the 1832 January and February issues of the *Millennial Harbinger*, in which Campbell wrote about the Turner insurrection, he said, "The last Assembly of Virginia has rendered itself memorable by many eloquent speeches which were made on the subject of slavery . . . but arose without passing a single law on the subject."[69] Campbell held the belief that the two greatest issues threatening the United States were slavery and Roman Catholicism. Through the years he wrote about both. Yet after 1847 his pessimistic mood began to shift during a trip he took to Europe, after which a renewed enthusiasm for the young republic he had left behind was evident once more. In a letter from Europe addressed to his daughter, he wrote, "I . . . often think of the hills around Bethany, and the enviable lot of those I left behind me, compared with that of the millions through which I am passing in this Old World. . . . May the Lord in his mercy watch over the destiny of your native country, and long preserve it from the vices and follies [of Europe]."[70] Notice here the contrast, common to the thought of the times, between the United States and Europe. The young republic is seen as a new creation in which the "vices and follies" of the old and decayed European world order are missing.

The image of the United States as a "new Israel" was one that was easily understood by those moving to conquer the western borderlands of the new nation. There was a sense of hope and mission as the United States spread across the continent. Hand-in-hand with this westward expansion went Protestantism, and within the religion of the republic was the sense of moving to become a millennial nation. The evangelist Lyman Beecher wrote in 1835 that "the millennium would commence in America," because with the successful revival the conversion of the entire world was now in prospect.[71] The fact that Alexander Campbell was able to adapt this millennialism to a changing frontier not only helped the Disciples to remain a permanent frontier reality but also greatly aided them in maintaining a continued growth that would lead them to become a vital religious body indigenous to the frontier of the United States.

The major change that Alexander Campbell made during this period of growth was a functional one in which he moved from a conception of "complete individualism to one that required cooperative organization and planning."[72] Just as the frontier was becoming more settled and moving toward organized community life, we find that Campbell and the Disciples in the 1840s and 1850s were also moving toward a more settled existence and relaxing their strict understanding of biblical essentials. During this period Campbell's focus was on "missions, education, culture, [and] the mission and destiny of [North] America."[73] Campbell began to combine the elements of restoration with human-made organization. He also placed millennial expectations in the context of the nation and a common national religion which was Protestant. Primitive Christianity would still remain the catalyst, the engine of the vision, but it was now possible to expand the biblical essentials to include educational institutions, Bible societies, and missionary organizations. These organizations would now become the tools used for conversion, tools that would both help conquer the minds and hearts of the nonbelievers and work against "Romanism." Further still, "[North] America, especially, and the Anglo-Saxon world, through its language, its Protestantism, and its civilization would become the missionary and benefactor among the nations ushering in the modern golden age."[74]

Campbell made a series of addresses that focused on his understanding of the favored status of the United States as a chosen nation, the destiny of the Anglo-Saxons, and the virtues of democracy. He advocated a common Christianity that was not only Protestant but also tied into the nation's identity and mission. In 1849 Alexander Campbell spoke to the Young Men's Mercantile Library Association of Cincinnati on "The Anglo-Saxon Language—Its Origin, Character and Destiny."[75] In this address Campbell traced the Anglo-Saxon people to the Old Testament Japheth, whose very name holds the promise of *enlargement*. Campbell explained how from this son of Noah, who populated the New World after the deluge with seven sons, came the people known as Anglos and Saxons.

Campbell described how the language of these people, which was now the mother tongue of the United States, reflected all that is good in this race. He wrote "that the mind and language of a people are commensurate; that the character of the one is essentially the character of the other."[76] He then summarized the impact and importance of the Anglo-Saxon language as well as its connection to religion. He boldly declared, "the Saxon language is the language of PROTESTANTISM."[77] In further describing the greatness of both language and people Campbell said,

> But, beyond all the advantages yet named, there is a power in our vernacular to extend itself by other means than natural generation. It is animated by a mighty proselyting spirit and power, arising from the innumerable stores of learning, science, art and new discoveries tied up in it—the rich behests of Anglo-Saxon genius. These are the great benefactors of man—the great reformers of the world . . . The Lord Almighty, who has now girdled the earth from east to west with the Anglo-Saxon people . . . by giving colossal power to Great Britain and the United States over the continents and oceans of the earth, will continue to extend that power and magnificence until they spread from north to south, as they have already from east to west, until, in one vernacular, in one language and with one consent, they shall, in loud acclaim and in hallowed concert, raise their joyful and grateful anthem . . . For all over the earth there will be but one Lord, one faith, one hope and one language.[78]

In 1852 Campbell gave another address entitled "The Destiny of Our Country"[79] before the Philo-Literary Society of Canonsburg College in Pennsylvania. Campbell again focused on the theme of a chosen nation that not only enjoyed divine favor, but also had before it a glorious destiny to fulfill. He wrote: "To us, He has given the new world and all its hidden treasures, with all arts and sciences of old. Europe, Asia and Africa look to Protestant America as a the wonder of the age, and as exerting a prepondering influence on the destinies of the world. We have, then, a fearful and glorious responsibility.[80] Campbell also extolled the virtues of education and of the educated mind. He said that while patriotism "has no place in the Christian religion,"[81] it could become a way to communicate the many blessings the nation had received. He concluded by saying,

> The United States of America, as they grow in learning, in the arts and sciences, and in all the elements of human wealth and power, can extend blessings to many nations; indeed to the four quarters of the world. In promoting her health, her wealth and greatness, especially that natural characteristic of a paramount regard for the freedom, amelioration, civilization, as well as evangelization of foreign lands, we pray for her prosperity . . . and advancement of the great family of man.[82]

Campbell not only demonstrated a renewed love and loyalty to the United States, he also emphasized that Protestantism was a divine tool for bringing forth the new world order that was part of his millennial theology.[83] It was a restored Protestantism, one that could purify and unify the church, that was to be the agent of change that Campbell wanted to see realized. And for Campbell "the Disciples were to pioneer in the union of all Christians by a complete restoration of the New Testament creedless church."[84] Yet that church was to function in the context of the United States. It was a church that expressed the religious identity of a nation, a nation that had received a special divine blessing which was to be shared with the other nations of the world. These were no longer apolitical millennial hopes but instead were hopes that saw the advancement of the cause of God as being intertwined with the advancement of the republic.

By 1860, with the prospect of war becoming more of a reality, Campbell's millennial hopes were diminishing. He wrote these words in 1864: "The times are full of corruption, and the church is contaminated with the times. We need to be reminded, in tones of tenderness, coming as from the world-renouncing agonies of the cross, that *we, the people of the living God are not of the world.*"[85]

Campbell had come full circle, returning to his ideal of the primitive church and the call to restoration, when the religion of the Republic failed to fulfill its promise. The Civil War brought great changes to the nation, which in turn divided Campbell's heirs, as those in the South continued to carry with them his earlier millennial hopes, while those in the North pursued the unity ideal.

4

The Disciples in Texas

Beginnings

Mexican Texas and the Tejanos, 1821–1836

The earliest European contact with Texas was made when Spanish explorers reached the Texas coastline in 1519. The conquistador Alabar Nuñez Cabeza de Vaca traveled across the southern part of Texas in the years 1530 to 1536. He was followed by Hernando de Soto's expedition, which crossed East Texas at about the same time Francisco Vásquez Coronado moved across the western panhandle in the 1540s.[1] When the Spanish first moved into Texas in the late seventeenth century they met the "Caddo-speaking peoples who inhabited the rolling woodlands between the Trinity and Red rivers in what is today eastern Texas and western Louisiana."[2] The name Texas comes from the Caddo word *Tejas*, which means "friends" or "allies," and was the name given the Caddo confederacy, the "Kingdom of Tejas."[3] Many other Native People in addition to the Caddos (or Caddohadacho) also inhabited this territory. The Cherokee Indians were the largest migratory tribe in Texas, but there were also villages of Shawnee, Alabama, Coushatta, Kickapoo, Delaware, Pascagoula, Lipan, Waco, Tonkawa, Tawakoni, Chickasaw, and Creek.[4] The Comanches, fierce warriors and a continuous threat to the Spanish settlers, were a nomadic people who did not have a centralized system of political authority as compared with the more settled hunter-gatherer groups.

Though life in the Texas borderlands was harsh for both Native Americans and the Spanish settlers, the contact between these races proved to be more unfortunate for the Native Americans because of the smallpox brought by the Spaniards.

Despite the decimation of the Native American population from disease, "Spain's goal . . . had not been the annihilation of Indians but rather their transformation into tax-paying Christians."[5] This may be surprising, especially given the slaughter of indigenous people by the Spanish sword that took place throughout the Americas during the sixteenth century. However several centuries later, Spain was busy building her empire in the Americas, and empire-building requires a tremendous amount of money. Whether from the earth (mines) or from citizens (taxes), revenue was needed. What this meant was that the primary purpose of the missions was to incorporate the indigenous people into the Spanish empire. More often than not, however, the paternalism of the Spanish missionaries led to the creation of "self-contained communities of Indians"[6] which did not advance the crown's plans. However, with the passage of time, and through intermarriage and acculturation, many Native People were unavoidably absorbed into Nueva España. "It also seems likely that in many places, [especially in the southwest borderlands], exposure to the market economy and the workaday world of Hispanic frontier society did more than the missions to alter [Native American] society and culture."[7]

Despite early Spanish explorations in the sixteenth century, the actual colonization of Texas took place much later, in the period from 1716 to 1731. Thus, Texas was one of the last provinces on the northern frontier occupied by Spanish settlers.[8] The first Spanish governor of Texas was Martín de Alarcón, who was named to his post in 1716.[9] One of the main tasks the Spanish government assigned Alarcón was to establish a "permanent settlement on the San Antonio River to serve as a halfway station between the [Río Grande] and East Texas."[10] Three permanent settlements were eventually established: one in Los Adaes in 1721 (near Natchitoches, Louisiana), one in La Bahía in 1722 (near Goliad, Texas), and San Antonio de Béxar in 1718 (modern San Antonio).[11] These became and remained the main centers for Spanish settlement in Texas throughout the eighteenth century.

When North American colonizers entered the borderlands of Texas they were crossing into a territory of contrasts and change. The borderlands people were Spanish by citizenship, and their language and religion was that of the crown. Though sparsely populated, the Texas borderlands was home to a Spanish frontier community that had developed its own economic structure and social divisions based "on immediate environment and local circumstances."[12] Because of the great geographical distance between these borderlands settlements and the seat of Spanish power in Mexico City, the concerns of the Tejanos were more immediate and regional.

The year 1821 marked the independence of Nueva España from Spain. The turmoil caused by the removal of the colonial yoke throughout the Spanish provinces was also felt in Texas. Division of loyalties, between those who were royalists versus those who were republicans, led to dissension and instability in the entire borderlands region. Those who supported Father Hidalgo's 1810 cry for independence, known as the "Grito de Dolores," joined forces and staged a military uprising in San Antonio de Béxar in 1811. This was led by a retired presidial officer named Juan Bautista de Las Casas. However, revolution was not all that was on Las Casas's mind. Instead he proceeded to confiscate property and cattle, to jail people, and to estrange many important citizens.[13] A counterrebellion ousted Las Casas and regained control of the town. For his impudence, crown officials in Coahuila shot Las Casas in the back for treason, decapitated him, and forwarded his head to Béxar so that the citizens could witness firsthand the punishment for taking up arms against royal power.[14]

In 1812 the people of Béxar welcomed the republican army led by Bernardo Gutiérrez de Lara, which was made up of Mexican and North American filibusters. In 1813 this republican uprising was crushed by royal troops led by General José Joaquín Arredondo. By incarcerating rebels, sequestering private properties, and arbitrarily executing suspected conspirators, the Spaniards had reasserted crown governance but further aggrieved the province's citizens.[15] Seeking to flee Arredondo's hostility, many of the oldest rancho families of the province made their way to Louisiana where they survived as common workers or remained with Texas Indian tribes for several years.[16]

The year 1821 marked the birth of the new Mexican republic, yet much that was Spanish was retained. The language, social divisions, and religion changed little, and Texas remained in many other ways Spanish. Consider the following two issues:

> Aspects of the Iberian legal tradition also endured, such as those pertaining to women. In Mexican Texas (1821–1836), a woman retained the title to property she held at the time of matrimony; in the United States during this same era, the newlywed surrendered any such possession to her husband. Wives, furthermore, laid equal claim to assets earned while married; gains made during the marital state became common property of the couple. . . . Customs protecting debtors similarly persevered. . . . Laws during the Mexican period in Texas acknowledged

a common man's rights to retain his tools, field animals, and even his land despite his indebtness.[17]

Not all that was kept from the years under Spanish domination, however, was either good or useful. Mexico also inherited all the problems of the old colonial regime. Two problems that demanded immediate attention were how to protect the Texas borderlands from illegal encroachment and how best to populate these territories. One of the pressing items on the agenda of the government of the new Mexican republic was promoting the settlement of the northern borderlands territory. The new government saw the repopulation of the Texas borderlands as a fundamental step in the region's recovery from all the turmoil of the 1810s. The key question remained, how best to do it. The Mexican government was well aware of the work previously done by the Spanish Cortes to create a Project for the Colonization of the Americas. However, because that project was presented and approved in June 1821, barely three months before Mexico gained her independence from Spain, it was never implemented. The plan contained two important articles, however, which the Mexicans later adopted. Roman Catholicism was declared the official religion of all settlers, and no slaves were to be brought into Texas; those who were brought in were to be immediately freed.

After independence from Spain, the Mexican government continued to deal with the Texas borderlands but did so now through the newly formed Committee on Foreign Relations. The members of this committee focused primarily on agrarian and colonization laws for the provinces of Texas and California.[18] The Mexican government knew that Texas needed to be preserved because of its importance and that no other means for accomplishing this remained except to populate it.[19] Utilizing the work already done by the Spanish Cortes of 1821, the committee presented a thirty-article colonization law in May 1822. This was then re-worked by the Colonization Committee, which issued a proposed final colonization law in August 1822. This law, however, was never enacted because Iturbide dissolved the Mexican Congress and then hand-picked a Junta Nacional Instituyente in November 1822.

Despite the changes in the politics of Mexico City, the provinces of Texas and Coahuila remained very concerned about their immigration and land issues. They were also under the direct pressure of the growing number of petitions for land grants that needed to be resolved. At least eleven empresarios were asking for permits to colonize in Texas, among them Haden Edwards, Daniel Stuart, and Arthur Wavell, who had first presented their petitions in 1822.[20] Despite the early dates of these permits to colonize, the first petition for colonization of Texas by North Americans was originally granted to Moses Austin in 1820, not by Mexico, but by the Spanish governor of Texas, Antonio Martínez. When Moses Austin appeared before Governor Martínez in 1820 he identified himself as "a native of the State of Connecticut, actually a resident of Missouri, a *Catholic*, a merchant and dealer in lead ore."[21] Austin's claim to Roman Catholicism is much more than a simple historical footnote. The 1798 Spanish constitution for all the provinces in Nueva España clearly established that "Liberty of conscience is not to be extended beyond the first generation; the children of emigrants must be catholic; and emigrants not agreeing to this must not be admitted, but removed, even when they bring property with them."[22] The mandate was clear. Immigrants to Spanish lands had to appear before officials to answer questions about their belief in the Roman Catholic Church. These questions when answered in the affirmative gave them full citizenship and declared their religious loyalty; in one oath, crown and church were both satisfied.

It is known that Moses Austin and his family moved in 1798 to St. Genevieve in Upper Louisiana, "the largest town in what would later become the Missouri Territory."[23] As subjects of the king of Spain and, in keeping with the recognized constitution of the Spanish territories, the Austins had been declared Roman Catholics. But it was not just that Mr. and Mrs. Austin were regarded as Catholic by the Spanish authorities. In a unique display of religious devotion, their son Jacques Elijah Brown Austin was baptized in the Catholic Church on July 13, 1804. When Moses Austin went to San Antonio de Béxar to make his petition to establish a colony in Spanish Texas, he was not only familiar with the Spanish emphasis on Roman Catholicism as a requirement for citizenship, but he could indeed correctly claim to have been a Catholic in Spanish territories. (This was irrespective of the fact that Moses Austin was born and baptized a Congregationalist and his wife an Episcopalian.) No doubt this claim of personal faith as demonstrated in the baptism of his youngest son helped Moses Austin get his land grant, but it is also indicative of something more.

The issue of religion in the Spanish and then Mexican borderlands was a multifaceted one. Mexican officials did not make it difficult for a foreigner to become a Roman Catholic, but it is clear that they expected the conversion of any prospective colonist.[24] However the temptation is to dismiss this insistence on a Catholic requirement because it was easily manipulated for the sake of convenience. Spain knew it could not force anyone to become a Roman Catholic. The questions asked of the newly arriving North American emigrants like Moses

Austin were in many ways perfunctory, as were the answers given by the non-Catholic immigrants. However the declaration that the Spanish borderlands were Roman Catholic presumed two important results for the Spanish crown. One was that a legal base had been clearly established by which it was possible to punish or remove any immigrant not abiding by Spanish law. The other was a legal attempt to foster the creation of a cultural-religious homogeneity among the population of the borderlands. This borderlands society was patterned after Spanish culture and Spanish Roman Catholicism, but also reshaped by its unique borderlands location.

But there was more. To talk about religion meant very different things to the Mexican Texan than it did to the Euro-American settler. The legal ruling on religion helped to establish a radical difference between the cultural worldview already in place in these borderlands and the cultural baggage the immigrants brought with them. As such, the religious difference between the Mexican Texan and the North American settler remained a constant irritant from 1821 to 1836. Historian Howard Miller has examined the great religious differences between the Euro-American settlers and the Mexican Tejanos they encountered in the borderlands. Miller says, "The existence of an established church may have been the feature that made Texas appear most foreign to Protestant—or even Catholic—[North] Americans. It is easy to forget how revolutionary—literally unprecedented—was the [North] American experiment in severing the timeless bond between priest and king, between church and state."[25] Moses Austin himself provides a clear example of how this different understanding of religion, which created conflict between Tejanos and North American settlers, was played out in Texas.

When Moses Austin submitted his original application for colonization in 1820 he "pledged only that his three hundred settlers would be industrious, loyal, and obedient to the Spanish government; he did not state specifically that they would be Catholic, or even Christian."[26] His skillful manipulation of the entire religion question was emulated by his son Stephen Fuller Austin, "who brought to Texas in 1821 an abhorrence of one of the defining characteristics of his native culture: intense denominational competition and intensely expressed religious sentiment."[27]

Stephen Austin was not so much anti-Catholic as he was anti-sectarian, distrustful of all clergy, and uncomfortable with any emotional display of religious sentiment. It is not surprising then that a continual complaint voiced against the North American colonists by the Mexican Tejano residents was the lack of respect the colonists showed the Roman Catholic faith of the borderlands resident. However, despite the tensions they generated, these religious differences were politically subordinated to the economic gains that both Mexicans and North Americans anticipated were to accompany the settling of the Texas borderlands.

The Spanish government granted Moses Austin permission to enter Texas with three hundred families and to inhabit "nearly one hundred and fifty miles square, which was bounded on the east by the Brassos [*sic*] river, and on the south by the Gulf of Mexico."[28] Moses Austin died shortly after receiving his grant, and it was his son Stephen who assumed responsibility for establishing the colony, as stipulated in his father's grant. As expected, the grant carried the clear "stipulation that the newcomers must be Roman Catholics or agree to become so before entering the country,"[29] which was something Austin was prepared to deal with. The grant also had a two-year time limit in which the land had to be made arable or the grant would be forfeited. The lands given to the settlers were exempt from taxation and duties for a period of seven years.[30]

Austin negotiated financial support for the settling of his colony from Colonel Joseph H. Hawkins of New Orleans for the amount of $4,000. For this investment Austin was prepared to give Hawkins "one-half interest in all lands granted Austin, "together with one equal half part of town lotts, emoluments, profits, monies, or effects derivable by the settlement and sale of the lands and lotts."[31] Stephen Austin set out for Texas with a small number of families, arriving in December 1821.

However, Texas had come under Mexican rule right before Austin arrived with his settlers. The Mexican revolution for independence from Spain had been a costly one, "with her population literally decimated (a tenth of the population, mostly young men of fighting age, had lost their lives)."[32] Mexico was a country in tremendous upheaval. So in 1822 Austin found it necessary to leave his colony under the care of Josiah Bell[33] and go to Mexico City to have the original Spanish grant confirmed by the newly established Mexican government. Returning in August 1823 Austin found his colony almost in ruins, but he had in his hands all the official documentation that established the legitimacy of his new colony.

Aware of the need to be frank with those interested in moving to Texas, and at the same time wishing to avoid any situations with the new Mexican government that would imperil his colonizing venture, Austin issued a circular letter dated October 30, 1823. In it he clearly defined the terms for settlement in his colony: "No one will be received as Settler, or even be permitted to remain in the country longer than is

absolutely necessary to prepare for removal, who does not produce the
most unequivocal and satisfactory evidence of unblemished character. . . . The Roman Catholic is the established religion of the Mexican
nation and the law will not allow of any other in this Colony."[34] Austin
was especially careful during the first years of his colony to avoid any
confrontations with Mexican authorities. His ultimate goal was the
colony's success.

> And Austin was at great pains to warn Protestant ministers who made
> inquiry about the establishment. He was especially stern with the Meth-
> odists. He warned the Reverend William Stevenson that any Methodist
> minister found preaching in the colony would be imprisoned, and he told
> his sister that he welcomed the Methodists' subsequent criticism of his
> firmness because it might help persuade the Mexican officials that he was
> doing all he could to enforce the law against Protestant worship.[35]

As was the case with Spain, Roman Catholicism remained the religion of the new Mexican republic. The Mexican Constitution of
1824 officially declared that, "The religion of the Mexican Nation is,
and will be perpetually, the Roman Catholic Apostolic. The nation
will protect it by wise and just laws, and prohibits exercise of any
other."[36]

In this same year the Mexican government officially made Texas y
Coahuila one state with the capital located at Saltillo. This was a protectionist move by the Mexican government to safeguard its borderlands from foreign control. By creating one state out of Coahuila and
Texas, the government was uniting a more stable state populated mostly
by Mexicans with one that was on the fringes of the nation with a very
mixed and transient population. There was much dissatisfaction with
this official decision, both from the Mexican Texans and North American settlers, and a conciliatory condition was eventually added to the
decision. The condition said that "as soon as the increase in [the Texas]
population should justify it, she should be disencumbered from the
alliance with Coahuila, and be permitted to take her place among the
Mexican sovereign states, on terms of perfect co-equality."[37]

Despite the harsh life in Texas, and the actual return to the United
States by some of Austin's settlers, Austin did establish the capital of
his colony and his personal home in the new city of San Felipe de Austin
on the eastern banks of the Brazos river. By August 18, 1824, Austin
"petitioned the supreme government, through the state authorities, for
permission to locate two or three hundred more families, specifying
that they should be 'industrious and of good morals' but [like his father]
saying nothing of their being catholics."[38] Austin, like the many other

U.S. *empresarios*, believed he could indeed establish additional successful colonies. A positive response from the Mexican government
to these requests was awaited.

The answer came in the 1825 colonization laws which were to be established by each individual state. On March 24, 1825, the state government of Coahuila y Texas passed a body of law "providing for the introduction of foreign settlers through the instrumentality of officers to be
called *Empressarios* [*sic*]."[39] These *empresarios* would in turn receive
"a compensation in lands proportioned to the number of colonists introduced by him."[40] Though the colonization laws of 1825 made no specific
mention of religion, they did make an important provision for the new
settlers. The laws of 1825 offered to foreigners "who come to establish
themselves in its territory, security for their persons and property, provided they subject themselves to the laws of the country."[41] The passing
of this law was a great achievement for Austin. In it he saw some guarantee that North American settlers would be offered protection without
having to actually become Roman Catholics. Austin had harbored the
belief that the new government of Mexico would eventually change its
position on Roman Catholicism as a prerequisite for settlement. In a letter
dated October 30, 1823, Austin wrote, "The Roman Catholic is the established religion to the absolute exclusion of all others and will continue for a few years, but the natural operation of a republic will change
that system."[42] Again we take notice of the difference in worldview held
by the Euro-Americans and the Mexican Texans. For the former a federal or republican system of government naturally meant religious freedom of choice. One would eventually lead to the second, and for this
not to happen was not only difficult for Americans to conceive but was
indicative of a serious problem.

Austin well knew that the issue of religion needed to be handled with
much prudence. He knew he needed to keep the incoming American
settlers satisfied while maintaining good relations with the Mexican
government. But Austin also knew there was another graver issue which
perhaps would prove more explosive than the religious one. That issue was slavery. It would indeed play a role in the movement to create
the Republic of Texas twelve years later. Austin wrote in 1824 to a
Mexican Texan in the state government who was a friend and ally of
the North American settlers:

> There are two obstacles which hinder imigration [*sic*] to this province
> and the whole nation: One is the doubt that exists concerning slavery
> and the other religion. Many catholics would come from Louisiana if
> they could bring and hold their slaves here. But as the larger part of
> their capital is in slaves, they cannot emigrate without bringing them,

and from the other States where there are not many catholics they will not come because there is not liberty of conscience. All would be content to pay for maintenance of the Catholic church if they could obtain the right of following the cult which they please.[43]

The use of slaves was crucial to the American settlers. If the Mexican authorities in Texas would not allow them the "liberty of conscience" to remain Protestants, they certainly were not going to also give up their slaves. So despite the efforts of the Mexican government to outlaw slavery, the Americans continually sought to circumvent these laws, even after the authorities outlawed the importation of slaves and gave freedom to the children born of slave parents on Mexican soil.

The issue of foreign settlement, which included the issues of religion and slavery, as well as the permit requests for land grants, became so pressing that the state of Coahuila y Texas passed the colonization law of 1825 even before completing its own state constitution. Once more Austin used his influence and the friendships of key Mexicans in the state legislature at Saltillo to help his colonization efforts. This time he called upon Baron de Bastrop, who had befriended Austin's father Moses and was now a willing and able ally.[44] While Article 3 of the laws of 1825 dealt with those who had "already arrived," Article 5 was directed at "new settlers," who were Austin's main concern. It was because of concern with the wording of Article 5 and what this would mean to new settlers that Austin called on his friends to help and help they did. Austin used his influence to ensure that the wording of Article 5 would not work against him. "As it appeared in the colonization law of 1825, Article 5 specified that . . . the new settlers, who present themselves to be admitted shall prove, by a certificate from the authorities of the place from which they came, their *christianity* and good moral character."[45]

The use of the word "christianity" was certainly a coup for Austin, because it was subject to such a broad interpretation. For the Mexicans, "christianity" was synonymous with Roman Catholicism, while for the American settlers it simply meant someone who professed some Christian belief. Given the upper hand in the lax wording of Article 5, it soon became common practice in the Austin colony to make available these certificates for the new settlers. They were issued from "the place from which they came," which was often either the office of the commissioner, who was Austin himself, or the office of the mayor a few yards away.[46] In addition to issuing certificates, Austin also promoted an outward show of loyalty to the Mexican government and its laws by his colonists. The new settlers not only swore to obey the constitution and laws of the Republic of Mexican states, but they also gathered around the Mexican flag and then saluted it (with or without gunfire). Austin thus maintained good relations with the state government all the while guaranteeing his uninterrupted colonization as *empresario*.

The Mexicans, however, were not unaware of, nor indifferent to, the great threat the Mexico-U.S. boundary posed as the number of North American settlers coming into Texas continued to increase. On April 15, 1824, José Antonio Saucedo, the political chief of Texas, advised Lucas Alamán, Mexican Secretary of Internal and Foreign Affairs, "that he was certain 'the United States was trying to annul or at least has the idea of annulling' the treaty of 1819 [Adams-Onís], and he believed the [North] American government would then assert its claim to the banks of the Río Grande.'"[47] Despite the early warnings from Mexican government officials and the suspicion about the United States' motivation to delay of the ratification of the Adams-Onís Treaty, North Americans continued to cross into Texas.

"By 1827 there were about twelve thousand [North] Americans across the Sabine."[48] With such a large North American population in Texas, conflict was unavoidable. Not only were the North American settlers flagrantly disregarding the avowal of religious loyalty and evading the controls put on slavery, but plans were soon underway by many of these colonists to separate Texas from Mexican control. The person behind an early ill-fated independence movement was a man named Major Benjamin W. Edwards.

Edwards was a friend of Austin's, whose brother Haden had received a land grant in 1825 near the town of Nacogdoches. But, unlike Austin, Edwards was less tolerant of Mexican law and less diplomatic in his dealings with the Mexican authorities. First he entered into conflict over the land titles of previous settlers, and then Edwards entered into dispute with the state authorities who accused him of usurping their power. In 1826 General Blanco banished Edwards from the province.[49] The rebels, however, had another plan of action in mind. "The reply of the dispossessed settlers was the organization of the ill-starred Fredonian Republic. This was led by Edwards, who drew the Cherokee Indians into his scheme by a proposal to divide Texas between the new State and the [Native People]."[50] Being a careful and astute *empresario*, Austin and his colony did not support the Fredonian revolt.

The Fredonian agitation however served as a brazen warning signal to the Mexican authorities. The Mexico City newspaper *El Sol* on July 29, 1829, was the first to issue a public warning that "the desire of the United States [is to] take Texas and Coahuila, as well as other border regions" and that "an invasion was imminent."[51] In November 1829, the editors of *El sol* were given a letter that Carlos María Bustamante had received, dated September 22, 1829, from Nicolás Bravo, who resided in New York.

> In his letter, Bravo urged that the national government 'open its eyes and provide remedies for the evils threatening Texas by the Anglo-Americans, who were trying to usurp it." Bravo, in his letter, stated that the United States had never been a friend of Mexico's and "never would be"; . . . [and that it wanted] Mexico's state of Texas to be united with the United States "either by purchase or by force." . . . Bravo also sent to Bustamante at the same time a kind of manifesto addressed to the Mexicans in which he included some United States newspaper clippings, with his comments on them.[52]

In 1829 General José Tornel persuaded President Vicente Ramón Guerrero to issue the Emancipation Decree, which abolished slavery in all of Mexico and forbade Americans from bringing any slaves into Texas. The Americans, however, resisted this ban on slavery, for even more important than the religious issue was their "keen interest in protecting their human investments."[53] The Americans claimed that their industry depended on slave labor. When the Mexicans continued to oppose slavery, Americans brought slaves in "under the fiction of indentured servants."[54] This ruse was developed by Austin himself, as the draft of a proposal he wrote to the Coahuila y Texas state legislature on March 31,1828, shows. Austin's proposed legislature would allow "those slave owners who were about to emigrate to Texas with their slaves to transform their relationship to one of master and bonded servant by a written agreement."[55]

As the province of Coahuila y Texas dealt with its immigration issues, the new Mexican republic faced successive upheavals in its government. On July 24, 1829, the Guerrero government confronted a new crisis when the Spaniards invaded Mexico, entering through Veracruz. This was followed by the Plan of Jalapa, which ended the government of Guerrero in December 1829. The need to provide for national security to defend from external threats in a time of so much internal disruption only highlighted the need to tighten control of the northern borders of Mexico in the Texas borderlands. On April 6, 1830, the secretary of foreign relations, Lucas Alamán, proposed a new colonization law which contained five major stipulations. It was the harshest colonization law to date for the Texas borderlands.

It stipulated not only that slaves were forbidden (again), but passports were now required for admission into Mexican territories, and independent settlers who were not on recognized land grants were to be ejected. Article 11 of the law of April 6 also prevented foreigners from settling along the borders of their own countries, which meant that Americans could not be legally introduced to any new colonies along the Mexico-U.S. border.[56] The federal Congress of Mexico "decreed that no more emigrants should come from the United States, except they hold permits from the Mexican consuls resident within those states."[57]

General Manuel Mier y Terán was sent by Mexico City to enforce this almost impossible immigration law. Terán, who was critical of the earlier policies that facilitated American settlements, wrote to Governor Viesca in 1831, saying, "It seems that in the town of Austin the decrees and orders of the government do not circulate, when they are contrary to the interests of said colony: but rather some orders are kept from the general public."[58] So much ill feeling was generated by the immigration law of 1830 that General Terán found it necessary to establish "twelve military posts in the hope of quieting the [North] Americans."[59] By 1833 this law had been abrogated by the Mexican government.

Tensions however were continually building in Texas. There was mounting dissatisfaction with the ever stiffening immigration laws, which seemed not only too confining to the Euro-American settlers but also more menacing. In addition, the creation in 1824 of the one state Coahuila y Texas from the two provinces had also been a "continual aggravation to the Texans." Again the main issue was that of control over use of the land." Coahuila was controlled by a majority of Mexicans, while Texas was not large enough to avoid being dominated by the larger native population of the two provinces."[60] The Americans decided to meet to discuss the state of the territories. A meeting was held in San Felipe de Austin on October 1, 1832, but because of poor attendance a second meeting was held in April 1833. At this second meeting Austin was sent to Mexico City to take the Mexican government the petition of the second convention. An integral element of the petition Austin carried with him called for a Texas statehood separate from the state of Coahuila.

Austin however found President Gómez Farías opposed to the statehood demand.[61] To the Mexican government, the notion of having a state on the Mexican-American frontier, self-governed mainly by Americans, may have seemed tantamount to surrendering Texas to the United States.[62] Disenchanted with Mexico's disregard for both his presence and petition, Austin "wrote a letter advising the settlers to proceed with forming a state. His letter was intercepted and he was arrested at Saltillo and detained in Mexico City until the summer of

1835, by which time he had become convinced of the futility of hoping for stable conditions in Texas from the operations of the existing Mexican government."[63]

When Austin returned to his colony in September 1835 he found a revolution already in the works.[64] From November through December 1835, Texan troops clashed with Santa Anna's forces at San Antonio de Béxar.

> Tejanos assisted the Anglo Texans in this early effort, both as militiamen and civilians. . . . Many of the families who had participated in the Mexican independence movement of the 1810s again aligned themselves with the concerns of the Texas region. On the other hand, numerous Tejanos, even among the social elite, sided with Mexico against the Anglo Texans. The majority of Tejanos, however, took a neutral stand on the hostilities.[65]

The gathering of troops at San Antonio de Béxar took place from February 24 through March 3, 1836, at one of its old missions, the Alamo. Colonel William Travis and the 200 American settlers and Tejanos who joined him were outnumbered by some 2,400–2,600 Mexican soldiers led by General Antonio López de Santa Anna. After more than an hour of combat the bloodshed had ended: all of the Alamo's defenders were dead and Santa Anna had lost some 500 to 600 men.[66] Weber discusses the symbolic significance some have given the encounter:

> The lore surrounding the battle of the Alamo provides the clearest examples of how the Texas rebellion, like so many major events, has been romanticized to take on meanings that transcend the event itself. . . . In certain kinds of history, and in [North] American popular culture, the Texas fight for independence has come to represent a triumph of Protestantism over Catholicism, of democracy over despotism, of a superior white race over a degenerate people of mixed blood, of the future over the past, of good over evil.[67]

This national lore is not just the product of contemporary historical interpretation; Stephen Austin, writing to a friend in May about the battle of the Alamo, had in just a few months developed a particular interpretive lens with which to analyze the meaning of what had taken place in San Antonio. He described the encounter as "a war of barbarism and despotic principles, waged by the mongrel Spanish-Indian and Negro race, against civilization and the Anglo-American race."[68]

After the Alamo, Santa Anna moved his troops to San Jacinto in East Texas. There the Mexican troops, now numbering 1,500, engaged Sam Houston's troops of 900, "which included a small company of Texas Mexicans led by Juan N. Seguín."[69] The defeat of the Mexican troops at the Battle of San Jacinto was not only a bloody one, but it meant that the tide had turned for the rebels. Within three weeks the Euro-American Texans "negotiated the Treaty of Velasco with Santa Anna wherein the defeated general conceded Texas independence and agreed to remove his army to Mexico beyond the Río Grande."[70] The Texas Constitution of 1836 proclaimed that all those living in Texas had automatically become citizens of the new republic the moment the delegates at Washington-on-the-Brazos had declared independence.[71] The Mexican Congress did not concede to the agreement, but there was no turning back. The Mexican province had been lost to the Euro-American settlers.

Religion in Texas: The Disciples' Beginnings

The history of the Roman Catholic Church in the Spanish empire of Nueva España is one of conflict and inner turmoil. After independence from Spain, the Mexican Roman Catholic Church "hoped to use independence as the occasion for escaping state control altogether by preventing any new government from assuming the patronato real [state power granted the Spanish crown over the church in the Americas]."[72] However, despite the conflicts and power struggles in and outside of the Church, right from the beginning of the Mexican republic Agustín de Iturbide's Plan de Iguala (1821) established the centrality and permanence of the Roman Catholic Church in Mexico. What this meant, writes Howard Miller, was that

> despite disruption and confusion, and throughout all the government permutations following Mexican independence, the basic statutory and constitutional position of the Catholic church, and the implications of that position for Anglo-Texans, remained the constant. There simply was no serious move between 1821 and 1836 to alter in any way the legal establishment of the church in Mexico. Its spiritual—if not economic—privileges were supported by virtually all Mexicans. Those privileges were stated concisely in the federal constitution of 1824 and were never altered throughout the period in which Texas remained a part of Mexico.[73]

In 1823 the federal Congress of Mexico enacted a law which stated that the government would see to it that "new towns are provided with a sufficient number of spiritual pastors."[74] In the constitution of the state of Coahuila y Texas it was further stipulated that, "The State shall regulate and pay all the expenses which may be necessary for the preservation of religious worship, in conformity . . . with the Holy See."[75] The salary for these "spiritual pastors" was to come from the new settlers themselves, which meant that the economic fortunes of the borderlands priests was a precarious one. Consequently, most priests earned a living through a variety of "secular endeavors" such as ranching."[76]

While the Franciscans "were the first to minister to the settlers on the frontier,"[77] by the early nineteenth century the spiritual welfare of the settlers in Coahuila y Texas was in the hands of the Bishop of Monterrey, who presided over the Diocese of Nuevo León. Under the Bishop were the priests at San Antonio de Béxar, Father Francisco Maynes, who was presidio chaplain, and Father Refugio de la Garza, who was parish priest.[78] These priests were charged with administering the sacraments and with the conversion of the "sectarians" (Protestants) in addition to endorsing the citizenship process of Euro-American settlers who sought to become Mexicans through marriage to a Mexican woman and then through conversion.[79] In 1823 Austin sought to secure the services of Father Maynes by means of a petition to the governor of Coahuila y Texas. He wrote that the people of the colony "if possible would like to have Father Maynes, chaplain of the company at Béxar and priest well known by many of them, who speaks English and French."[80] Despite the approval of Austin's request, "no priest visited the Austin colony before 1832."[81] The religious neglect of the colonists was a consequence of the disarray of the Mexican church after independence from Spain, which was largely due to political issues and concerns:

> The largely Spanish episcopate loyally returned to Spain after Mexico won its independence, and the Vatican, which refused to recognize Mexican independence until 1836, refused to make new appointments. By 1829 there were *no* bishops in all of Mexico. There was no archbishop in Mexico from 1825 until 1840. There was no bishop in Monterrey . . . which included Texas, between 1821 and the Revolution of 1836. On the eve of that revolution, there were two secular priests in all of Texas.[82] Given the disorder evident in the Mexican Roman Catholic Church after 1821 it can be said that "it was lay devotion, not its wealth, that saved it."[83]

The reactions of the North American colonists who contacted Austin about settling in Texas varied. While some expressed concern about the Catholic Church, "the majority of requests for information about Austin's colony emphasized considerations of a practical nature and did not mention religion at all."[84] Of greater interest to the colonists, many of whom were from the South, was the slave issue. As Miller reports, one Mississippi slaveholder informed Austin in 1825 that any limitations on the rights to have slaves in Texas would "'check the tide of emigrating *spirits* at once.'"[85]

> Just as Austin and his colonists did not protest the religious establish-
> ment in the early years of the colony, neither did Austin devote very
> much of his time and energy to the matter of religion in the struggling
> colony. The subject of religion is most notable for the infrequency with
> which it appears in his public and private correspondence.... When
> Austin did address the subject of religion, it was usually ... to remind
> prospective colonists—especially pestiferous preachers—of the
> [Roman Catholic]establishment. [86]

For Austin and his settlers, the fact that the Catholic Church did not
send priests did not greatly concern them. Some of this had to do with
the disdain most colonists (and Austin)[87] felt for Catholicism, and some
of this had to do with the fact that despite the Mexican government's
exclusion of any other faith that was not Catholic, Protestant ministers could not be kept out of Texas.

The arrival of Protestantism in Texas began as early as 1816 in the
Euro-American colony of Jonesboro near the Red River, which pre-
dated Austin's colony by seven years.[88] In that year a Methodist minister named William Stevenson began preaching in the home of a
Mr. Wright. In 1817 he organized a church, and in 1818 a camp meeting was held.[89] In 1820 the group of thirty families which accompanied Moses Austin on his journey from Missouri to Louisiana included
three preachers: Joseph L. Bays, a Baptist, Martin Parmer, a Methodist, and Bill Cook, a Universalist.[90] While waiting at the Texas-
Louisiana border for Moses Austin to return from San Antonio de
Béxar, all three men preached. Then, in a bold move, Bays held a three-
day meeting at the home of a Mr. Hinds some eighteen or twenty miles
from San Augustine in Texas territory. In 1823, while Austin was in
Mexico City, the same Rev. Bays held services at San Felipe de Austin.
He was arrested by order of the governor, though he managed to escape from the Mexican authorities.[91]

Austin, ever so careful not to jeopardize the future of his *empresario*
career, was much chagrined at all this "sectarian" activity in the new
colonies. In 1824 Austin sternly warned the Rev. William Stevenson
that "if a Methodist, or any other preacher, except a Catholic, was to
go through the country preaching I should be compelled to imprison
him."[92]

That same year he also expressed his concern to his sister when he
wrote that a "few fanatics and imprudent preachers at this time would
ruin us."[93] But the advent of Protestantism was not to be easily stopped
by Austin or the Mexican authorities. The situation was a difficult one
given the absence of Catholic clergy and the active presence of Protestant preachers. Many of these preachers did not bother to consult with

Austin or to ask his permission to establish Protestant worship activities. Austin was especially concerned about the vigorous activities of the Methodists. In a letter to his friend Josiah Bell, dated 1824, he described the Methodist preachers as "too fanatic, too violent and too noisy."[94] Austin also wrote, "The subject of preaching must be managed with prudence, for I do assure you that it will not do to have the Methodist excitement raised in this country. All this is for your eye, and your confidential friends, and not for the public indiscriminately."[95] The Protestants' presence, however, was only to become more visible and more active:

> The first Sunday school in Texas was established in 1829 but when the suspicions of the Mexican authorities were aroused, Austin closed the Sunday school. Several other Sunday schools were established in 1829 and 1830, however, and continued to function. A Cumberland Presbyterian colporteur reached Texas by 1829 and began an energetic itinerary of delivering Bibles and religious literature to all [Euro-]American colonies, carrying with him the Spanish Bibles for the Mexican population as well. This is apparently the first record of any Protestant minister interesting himself in the spiritual welfare of the Mexican people in Texas.[96]

With the Methodists and Baptists already settled in Texas by the early 1830s, the westward-moving Disciples of Christ were not far behind. The earliest known group of settlers of the Disciples of Christ movement to enter Texas "migrated from Kentucky, in 1824, under the leadership of Collin McKinney.[97] Collin McKinney had been a Freewill Baptist but "came into contact with the preaching of Barton W. Stone, and some time before the year 1823 identified himself with the Restoration movement while a resident of Kentucky."[98] The group later discovered that due to the imprecision of the survey lines they originally had settled in what is today western Louisiana. However in 1831 "they made sure they were in Texas, for they not only settled on Red River, at a crossing that came to be known as McKinney's Landing . . . but they promptly joined in the moves for a Revolution against the Mexican government.[99]

That these early Texas Disciples would almost immediately join in the North American settlers' push for independence from Mexico is not very surprising. The McKinney clan, with so many other Euro-American settlers who came to Texas in the early decades of the nineteenth century, were part of what seemed an almost unstoppable wave of human migration moving westward in their search for land. And their movement had tremendous geopolitical as well as religious repercussions. These Protestant settlers were in a true sense culturally bound. This is evidenced by how quickly they expressed their political unhappiness with the Mexican government in a theological language that united all North American Protestants against Mexican Roman Catholics. It was now stated that Methodists, Baptists, and Disciples were involved in that

> age-old struggle between religious bigotry and freedom, . . . Santa Anna, the priest, the enemies of constitutional liberty throughout Mexico, will tremble when they learn that the blood and treasure of thousands of descendants of that patriotic band of heroes, who triumphed over England in the days of her strength and pride, have been tendered us in our present struggle for liberty and free institutions.[100]

Collin McKinney became one of the signers of the Texas Declaration of Independence of 1836. He was elected to serve in the Congress of the new Republic of Texas representing Red River County, which is today North Texas. So it was that the Disciples of Christ, by their move into Texas, became a part of that force which forever altered these borderlands.

Another group that identified themselves with the Disciples movement also entered Texas shortly after the McKinneys in 1836. These settlers were from Alabama, Mississippi, and Tennessee, and they were accompanied by two Disciples ministers, Lynn D'Spain and Mansil W. Matthews.[101] This group came in search of free land in Mexico. Their caravan was accompanied as far as Memphis by David Crockett and finally arrived in Fort Clark (Clarksville) in January 1836,[102] where Lynn D'Spain's oratory made quite an impression. Carter Boran describes D'Spain as "one of the most outstanding and powerful preachers of his day":

> He made a great name for himself before he came to Texas. He was not only a great preacher but he was an effective teacher . . . in addition to his preaching to the little Clarksville group, he also conducted a school for the settlers' children. . . . He was among the first planters of the seed of the Kingdom in Texas.[103]

After the battle of San Jacinto, the group at Clarksville disbanded, moving into other parts of Texas.

The years 1841–1842 marked the beginning of what was to be the first "Christian Church" in East Texas. Its founder was C. Gates, a Disciple from Indiana who wrote about this new congregation in the May 1842 edition of the *Millennial Harbinger*. In the article Gates mentioned the support given to him by the now elderly Collin McKinney and his family. This was the fourth[104] organized congregation of the Disciples in Texas, none of which was "continuous."[105] The movement of people during this westward expansion made it difficult for newly formed congregations to become stable. This is what happened with the McKinney families who, in search of better and richer land, moved into what is today Van Alystine. At this new site, in September of 1846, the families helped to organize what has become the oldest continuous Christian church in Texas, located on the border of Grayson and Collins counties, and originally called Liberty Church.[106]

The informal structure of the Disciples movement did not provide for keeping records and minutes. As a result, knowledge of Disciples history in Texas during this early period before the Revolution of 1836 is quite fragmentary. For example, in addition to what is known about the McKinneys, Matthews, and D'Spain, there is a letter to Barton Stone dated 1833 from a C. C. Defee, who had migrated from North Carolina with his family and lived in the Dezavalos Colony in Grande Saline, Texas. Defee makes a plea to Stone: "I am alone here and the *only one* that stands up for the Christian faith. . . .Try to persuade some good and faithful preacher to come and assist me . . . "[107] Like Defee, there may have been many others involved in the Disciples movement in Texas when it was still a province of Mexico, but, again, the frequency of movement of these North American settlers as well as the loose structure of the newly emerging Disciples movement did not aid the keeping of accurate records.

As an indigenous frontier religious movement, the Disciples of Christ often merged their understanding of the Gospel and zeal for evangelism with the reality of the frontier in order to carry on their ministry. For example, some Disciples were circuit riders who also tended to their farms, while others not only preached to the North American frontier population but also gave them a secular education. Using open platforms or tents, these early Disciples in Texas preached in the midst of what were often difficult circumstances. In the face of the harsh borderlands way of life, the Disciples remained true to their heritage, which was characterized by "empiricism, common sense, democracy, and practical religious faith."[108] Because of this, their preaching was practical and not filled with sentimental ideas. This preaching often placed them at odds with the more fervent Methodist and Baptist frontier pastors:

> In almost every community the reformers were inveighed against by preachers of other sects, were refused buildings for public worship, and every newly organized group was set apart as an object of contempt. . . . They were known by the epithet, "Campbellism," and the appellation spelled anathema.[109]

Yet despite the controversy and opposition, by 1860 the Disciples churches in Texas numbered fifty-three with about 2,500 members.[110]

In 1886 the Disciples of Christ in Texas created a state organization called the State Convention after holding a series of informal "co-operation meetings" which had begun as early as 1850. The Disciples' organization covered the geographical zone "north and south from the Red River to the Gulf of Mexico, and a distance east and west from the Sabine River to Corpus Christi, within one hundred and fifty miles of the Río Grande River."[111] In the same year that the state convention was established, the Texas Missionary Society was also created. Monies were now set aside for missionary efforts, evangelists were hired for new church starts, and the Disciples of Christ in Texas moved toward more efficient organization. As the Disciples continued to grow and move into their second phase of development after 1886, the center of most congregational activity for Disciples in this large geographical area remained northeastern Texas.

5

A View from the Twenty-first Century

History from the Borderlands: Tejano Disciples

Early Decades of Work: 1899–1925

Churches Started:	San Antonio (1899)
	Sabinal (No Date)
	El Paso (No Date)
	Martindale (1907)
	Lockhart (1908)
	San Benito (1912; Closed 1916)
	Robstown (1914)
Community Organization:	Mexican Christian Institute (1913)

The very scant and meager records that tell about Disciples work among Mexican-Texans point to San Antonio as the site for the first meeting. The Disciples' newspaper *The Missionary Tidings* reported in October of 1888 that a Disciples Mexican mission had been started in San Antonio and was doing "prosperous work with its feeble support."[1] However, this mission was not originally intended to be a church started for the Mexicans living in San Antonio. The article also asked "if [this mission were] pushed to success, what might be its possibilities in spreading the pure Gospel into Mexico . . . ?"[2] The primary goal of the mission was to spread the Disciples movement further south into Mexico, which the Disciples did accomplish at Juarez in 1895. It is not surprising then that this first attempt at work with the Tejanos of San Antonio was described as "weak"; there is no further mention of it until 1899.

By this time the American Christian Missionary Society was under the leadership of Secretary George B. Ranshaw. He visited San Antonio in the spring of 1899 and learned of a group of Mexican-Texans who "were seeking larger religious liberty."[3] Ranshaw visited this group and through an interpreter not only preached but also baptized a few of them. While records do not say who Ranshaw's interpreter was, the fact that Ranshaw assigned and left Y. Quintero as the organizing pastor for this first Mexican-Texan Disciples congregation might mean that Quintero was at that first gathering. The early records do not say who Y. Quintero was or where he came from.[4] However, given the great success of the Disciples missionary efforts begun in Monterrey in 1897, it may well be that Quintero was a product of the missionary work in that city. Quintero's assignment to work in San Antonio, however, was much more than just putting to good use the human resources being developed by the Euro-American missionaries in Mexico. The presence of this first Mexican native assigned to serve the Disciples missions to Mexican Texas presaged the beginning of a dependence on Mexico for leadership in Texas. Records show that in June 1899 the American Christian Missionary Society began to provide financial support to the San Antonio Mexican mission.

Under the aegis of the Texas Christian Missionary Society, 1903 and 1904 were years of expansion and growth for the Anglo Disciples. In only two years, 64 churches and 42 Sunday schools had been started; 32 church houses erected; more than $57,000 in cash had been received, and there was a gain of 7 percent to the Disciples membership rolls.[5] This early period of increased internal organization and statewide growth was followed by the leadership of J. C. Mason as State Secretary of the Texas Christian Missionary Society (1904–1914). Again, this was a time of much growth for the Disciples throughout the state, which was reflected in the organization of fourteen districts, each with its own district board and district evangelist. The goal was to promote greater efficiency in the missions work of the Texas Christian Missionary Society (TCMS) by facilitating the work of the district evangelists with pastorless churches. "The gradually growing successful operations of district work produced much enthusiasm which extended to the proposal . . . For organized state work."[6]

Mason's tenure is described by Disciples historian Carter E. Boren as the "renaissance" of the society. The TCMS became better organized and more systematic in its operations, but Mason also wanted the Texas Disciples to begin to intentionally address the changes that were taking place throughout the state. In his annual address as state secretary in 1906, Mason shared his concerns about the voids in missions work that Disciples were still not dealing with adequately. Mason's first concern had to do with the cities. He wrote:

> One-third of our entire population live in the cities. Our best young people from the country today will be the business men and women of the cities in a short time. San Antonio, Houston, Dallas, and Galveston are growing wonderfully. El Paso has also made a marvelous growth. What are we doing to keep pace in Christian work, with this marvelous growth?[7]

Mason was also concerned with the increased number of foreign immigrants arriving in Texas.

> No part of our great country is adding to its population more rapidly than Texas. . . . Foreign immigration is coming, 1,026,499 last year [1905], these in a short time, to become citizens, must be trained for Christian citizenship, or become a menace to our peace and happiness . . . the sturdy German, already well educated in the German way, can be trained into a splendid American-Christian citizen. The best teacher of the Mexican is a true, trained and faithful Mexican. . . . We need training schools for ministers and for missionaries.[8]

Mason's concern with foreign immigrants was voiced in the language of manifest destiny and his call for the support of the education and theological training of non-Americans, Tejanos, for Christian ministry was quite accurate. Unfortunately, providing for this fundamental need in Texas missions work was never taken very seriously. Mason, who supported Disciples work with Tejanos, knew of the great need that existed for trained leaders and for materials in Spanish. However no one could foresee the great injury the neglect of this crucial area would have on the overall missions work of Disciples with Mexican-Texans. Even today, after more than ninety-five years, leadership development continues to be the most neglected area in the work of Disciples among the Tejanos in Texas.

Despite the slow progress in missions work with Mexican-Texans, Mason did report in 1906 the existence of three Mexican missions, though he gives no dates for when they were actually begun. In San Antonio, Mason reported that the Mexican mission had a "missionary's home and a place for worship."[9] He credited Ignacio Quintero (called "Y. Quintero" in another report) with "making some headway against the superstition, sectarianism and the sin in a populous and wicked part of the city."[10] In El Paso, Mason reported the need to financially

undergird the work of pastor J. M. Martínez, whose small congregation was meeting in cramped quarters. Mason makes this plea: "When
I tell you that [Martínez] pays house rent and hall rent and supports
his family on less than $40 per month, you will agree with me that he
needs a home for himself and the mission. We must buy property for
this mission if we are to see it succeed. Here is the opportunity for some
of our people of means to plant. . . . "[11]

The third mission was in Sabinal, under the leadership of F. B.
Martínez,[12] "where the Mexican Church owns an adequate building and
is making the best growth of any of these churches."[13] In 1907 a report
in the January issue of *Texas Missions* adds to the list of Mexican
missions one in the town of Martindale, led by Julius Salinos [Julian
Salinas] who held "regular services and Sunday school."[14] However,
the Martindale mission is only mentioned once again, in 1912, after
which it seems to disappear.[15] It is possible that Salinas also started
work at Lockhart in 1908, as a preaching point, which outgrew the
mission at Martindale and led to its closing after 1912. This may help
to explain why the Lockhart Mexican-Texan congregation continues
to be mentioned in various reports beyond 1921.[16]

In 1908 work was reinitiated at the first site in San Antonio. What is
interesting about this second attempt to start a Mexican-Texan church
in San Antonio is that this effort originated, not with the Texas Christian Missionary Society, but with the Disciples missionaries in Mexico.
Juarez had been the site of the first Disciples missionary work in
Mexico,[17] but in 1897 the work was transferred to Monterrey, "this being
deemed a more strategic point and also more healthful."[18] In 1905,
Samuel Guy Inman (1877–1965), who was to become the most vocal
and respected Disciples advocate for Latin American missions on an
ecumenical level, began his period of service in Monterrey.

Inman had been originally assigned to work with the English-speaking
congregation in Monterrey, but in March 1908 he was transferred to
serve as the superintendent of the newly created board in the State of
Coahuila and Southern Texas.[19] The decision to give over the manage-
ment of Mexican missions work in Texas to the Christian Woman's
Board of Missions was reported in the August 1908 issue of *Texas
Missions.*[20] Inman moved his headquarters to Ciudad Porfirio Díaz
(now called Piedras Negras), closer to the Texas border, and in that
same year, he and his Mexican assistant, Felipe Jiménez, went to San
Antonio.

By 1908 the Mexican church started by the Disciples in 1899 was
no longer meeting.[21] In response to the closing of this mission in a city
with so many Mexican-Texans, Inman and Jiménez "rented a building

on South Laredo Street, and held a meeting of a month's duration. This meeting resulted in the reorganization of the church [started in 1899] with fourteen members and the organization of a Bible school with fifteen enrolled. Manual [*sic*] Lozano of Monterrey, Mexico, became the pastor of the newly organized church."[22] After the reorganization of the South Laredo Street church at the end of the first decade of the twentieth century, the Disciples had only five Mexican-Texan missions in Texas, in San Antonio, El Paso, Sabinal, Martindale, and Lockhart. These five missions were the result of twenty years of Disciples work, from 1888 to 1908.

When reviewing the history of these early Disciples Mexican-Texan missions, a very significant practice stands out. In all the new missions, the Disciples ministers assigned to be pastors to these congregations were from Mexico, no doubt graduates of the Disciples schools run by the missionaries.[23] This dependence upon Mexico to provide the leadership for the Disciples churches of Texas has been highly detrimental to the education and development of indigenous Mexican-Texan Disciple leaders. Relying on the educational work of the Disciples missionaries in Mexico to prepare Spanish-speaking ministers, the Disciples did not feel the need to provide for such training in Texas itself. In trying to understand the mentality that produced this appalling void in their leadership preparation, a telling indicator was the 1908 decision to give the missions work of southern Texas over to the Christian Women's Board of Missions.

The Christian Women's Board of Missions had been organized in 1874 for "world-wide evangelization and education," claiming to be "neither home missions nor foreign missions, for it is both."[24] However, the fact that the work in Texas would be supervised from Mexico, by a Disciples missionary assigned as an overseas worker, leads one to conclude that the work with Mexican-Texans was seen as "foreign" missions work, even if it was done within U.S. borders. The crux of the problem was that the Texas Disciples truly perceived the Mexican-Texans as Other, as outsiders, as foreigners. Support for this conclusion can be found in the articles about the work with Mexicans in Texas that were written during the first two decades of the 1900s. For example, the October 1905 issue of *Texas Missions* contains this call for help:

> We have a large Mexican population in Texas. Preachers are ready to preach the gospel to them in their own language. Bro. L. C. Brite has offered to be one of four persons to support a *native* missionary and mission. No one has yet responded. Bro. Brite has gone right on aiding J. M. Martínez and the El Paso Mission. Who will help?[25]

Notice that the call was for a "*native* missionary" which is what J. M. Martínez was. Ironically, it was L. C. Brite who would later provide the funds for the founding of the Disciples seminary in Fort Worth, Brite Divinity School, yet his important financial support during this early phase of Mexican-Texan missions work went to support ministers from Mexico. There was no demonstrated concern by Texas Disciples for the training of Tejano ministers, even though leaders like Mason and others realized there was a pressing need and had verbalized their concerns.

It is almost inconceivable that the leaders of the missions work among Mexican-Texans could not envision the impact that the lack of indigenous leadership would have on the future of Disciples work in Mexican-Texan communities. Perhaps there was an underlying assumption that Mexican-Texans were not capable of completing an educational program for ministry. Perhaps their perceived status as outsiders and foreigners was understood by the Disciples to mean that they were not interested or reluctant to become the leaders of Mexican-Texan Disciples congregations. Perhaps the Disciples felt too uncomfortable working with Mexican-Texans in the borderlands and were ambivalent about the work that needed to be done. A very interesting article appeared in the February 1920 issue of *World Call.* The author, Lewis P. Kopp, was reporting on the work the Disciples were doing among the Euro-Americans in the Río Grande Valley. He mentions the churches at Mercedes, McAllen, and Harlingen, but when he gets to Brownsville, he makes this observation. "The conditions are different in Brownsville, it being right on the border. It is practically a 'foreign mission field.' With a population of 17,000, only about 3,000 are Americans, the rest being Mexican or Spanish. There are only about 1,000 non-Catholic persons"[26] There is no mistaking the tone of the statement: These "Mexicans or Spanish" are not like us Disciples, they are not American and they are not Protestant. Whatever the underlying factors may have been, what cannot be denied is that Mexican-Texans were perceived as outsiders and Other. This is made clear in the variety of missionary newspapers.

The Disciples' work among Mexican-Texans continued to be hard and slow. In the years 1908 to 1912 there were no new additions to the five Mexican-Texan Disciples missions already in existence and there is no further mention of the church in El Paso. It seems to have closed during this four-year gap. The November 1912 issue of the *Missionary Tidings* contained the following general observation about the work in Texas: "Our five churches in Texas have a hard field to cultivate. The people are *roving* and often *ignorant* and *irresponsible.* So far our work is extremely unsatisfactory in Texas. We need to devote much more time to this work."[27]

Despite the clear statement of the need to invest more time and resources, it would be another four years until the start of the Mexican Church in Robstown, Texas, in 1912. This new church start was the result of a visit by Dr. W. A. Alton, a Disciples missionary in Monterrey, who was visiting Texas with his family. While at Robstown, he "gathered together a congregation of Mexicans at the Baptist Church" since he found "there was no religious service of any description for them in this town."[28] The Robstown church was reported as officially being organized in 1914, the year it began to receive financial help from the Christian Woman's Board of Missions. In support of the Robstown mission, the CWBM made a loan for the purchase of a building and also helped to support the minister, Mauricio Alonzo.[29]

Alton's visit to Texas in 1912 also served as the catalyst for the formation of the mission in San Benito. This was the first Mexican-Texan mission for the Disciples in the Río Grande Valley.[30] What is grievous about this new church start effort was that it took place sixty-two years after the founding of the first Presbyterian Mexican-Texan church in that same city. Two years later, in 1914, the church in San Benito, led by Pilar Silva, was reported to have purchased a lot in the hope of erecting a church building within the year. However, *Missionary Tidings* reported problems: "This congregation fluctuates in number of membership owing to nearness to the border and this makes the work more difficult. Even this difficulty has its compensations as the new members return to Mexico with a knowledge of the Gospel and can preach it to others."[31] The Disciples work in San Benito was last mentioned in the 1916 issue of *Missionary Tidings*. "The work here has suffered practical annihilation through continued border disturbances. Pilar Silva held tenaciously to his post and endeavored to hold up the work, but all in vain, so at present plans are being arranged for his transfer to another field."[32]

What the report referred to as "border disturbances" was the Mexican Revolution (1910–1921), which began with the overthrow of the dictatorship of Porfirio Díaz. At the core of the Mexicans' discontent was the unequal distribution of land.[33] When the new government of Francisco Madero failed to solve the agrarian crisis, Emiliano Zapata and his chiefs issued their *Plan de Ayala* in November 1911. When this plan for land redistribution was met with military action by the Madero government, fighting broke out throughout the country. For a decade, from 1910 until December 1920, when Alvaro Obregón became the constitutional president, Mexico lived through years of great political upheaval, economic crisis, and bloody turmoil.

The long years of the Mexican Revolution caused many problems for the Protestant missionaries of all denominations both in Mexico and along the Texas-Mexico border.[34] The November 1916 issue of *Missionary Tidings* reports the negative impact of the revolution on more than half of the Mexican-Texan Disciples congregations.[35] Work was either weakened or temporarily suspended or permanently halted in the three towns of Robstown, San Benito, and Lockhart. In San Benito, the pastor Pilar Silva was transfered and the church was closed.[36] The pastor of Robstown, Mauricio Alonzo, was also transfered to San Antonio due to "adverse conditions brought on by the war situation and the local famine in that section."[37] However, unlike San Benito, the Robstown church was reopened within the year under the new leadership of Pastor José Cueva.[38] The church in Lockhart was also in great economic need; it was reported that the pastor "Julian Salinas labors on, receiving only sufficient wages for the barest necessities of a meager subsistence for himself and his wife."[39]

By 1919 the presence of Mexicans in Texas, and in all the U.S. borderlands, was being referred to as the "Mexican problem" in the Disciples newspapers. This reaction was no doubt due to the great migration of Mexicans who, fleeing the war, had moved into the southwest borderlands of the United States.[40] The following article appeared in the September 1919 issue of *World Call.* It was written by E. T. Cornelius, who was to become superintendent for Mexican missions in Texas for the United Christian Missionary Society, which had been organized in 1920.

Almost every phase of the immigrant question in the United States has been fully treated with the exception of the *Mexican problem* of the Southwest. . . . It is impossible to know at this time the actual number of Mexicans to be found in the various parts of the United States. . . . The Mexicans living in the United States may be divided into two general classes. First, those who have lived in this country for many years . . . The second class, the strictly immigrant class. . . . We may truly say that a small percentage of them has become truly American citizens. . . . It is needless to say that when these people came to the United States, they did not suddenly forget or leave behind their former modes of living, their vices, their superstitions and their *nonreligion.* . . . They are a *primitive* people and live under conditions quite different from our own people. . . . The Christian forces of this country should realize the great importance of the work that needs to be done among these Mexican people within our borders and the responsibility that is theirs for the *Americanization* and *Christianization* of these many thousands of *strangers* within our borders.[41]

Cornelius's article is followed by another examination of Mexicans in Texas. This article, written by an unnamed Disciples missionary, appeared in the November 1920 issue of *World Call*. This second article stated that

> there are approximately 1,500,000 Mexicans and Spanish-Americans in the United States, with an increase which has been very great during the war and the troublesome times in Mexico. Texas has the largest number. . . . The largest single colony is at San Antonio, Texas, with about 500,000 . . . Many of these people are in a very destitute condition, live in crowded, unsanitary quarters and become ready victims of disease and crime. Large numbers are illiterate; the majority of them do not speak English; many are positively *un-American*.[42]

Given the tone and content of these denominational pieces, it is not surprising that the development of Mexican-Texan missions was so slow and uneven. The tragic irony is that in Texas, by the turn of the century, there were more than one million Mexicans or people of Mexican descent. Yet the articles written by the leaders of missions work to Mexican-Texans describe this population group in disapproving and disparaging language.

This makes one pause and ask the following questions: How does a missionary society propose to motivate congregations to provide the necessary funding for work among people whom that missionary society so obviously believes are inferior and almost beyond help? Can missions leaders really convince congregations that a wise missions investment would be for them to give funds for work among people who are described as "un-American"? If these people are as different from the Texas Disciples as described in the articles, why should the Anglo Disciples congregations help them in the first place?

The glaring contradictions in the work of Disciples among Mexican-Texans are overwhelming. The ambivalence, though never stated, is always present between the lines. The Disciples seem to be caught between their heritage of evangelistic work going back to Walter Scott and Cane Ridge. Yet they were also a people shaped by the ethos of the North American frontier. As such, their cultural/social reality was that of North Americans living in the borderlands where being non-Caucasian was a sign of inferiority. While the Texas Disciples seemed to possess a foundational grasp of a broad theology for missions, one which understood that the Church was called to serve all people, this understanding was lived out in constant tension with the culture, which was racially conscious. The reason this tension existed was because the Disciples also possessed a foundational *perception* that the people they are called to serve were inferior, they were not really North American, and they were not really Christian.

Perhaps this helps to explain the continual support given by the denomination and private donors to the Mexican Christian Institute in San Antonio. The support given to the Mexican-Texan mission in that city, and to the others throughout the state, was never comparable. What was important about the creation of the Mexican Christian Institute was that it provided the Texas Disciples a way to assume the role of benevolent giant as opposed to that of humble servant. Given the many layers of manifest destiny ideology so prevalent during this time, the important task of "civilizing and Christianizing " inferior "strangers" was a role the Disciples understood. This role was very much in keeping with how Protestant North Americans perceived their place in the borderlands and in the world. The Texas Disciples were simply fulfilling their obligation as both patriotic U.S. citizens and as good Christians.

So while the Disciples continued to moved tentatively to start new churches around the state, the city of San Antonio became the center of focus for a clearly defined mission to the Mexican-Texan population. In 1913 the Christian Woman's Board of Missions purchased a lot and approved the funding for the construction of a building with an auditorium, a gymnasium, and a home for the missionary in charge.[43] The building was to house the Mexican Christian Institute (though today it is called the Inman Center) and was dedicated in November 1913. The institute served the Mexican-Texan community of San Antonio through a variety of social ministries. In June 1913 a free medical clinic with milk and ice for babies was opened; in April 1915 a kindergarten was opened; and a day nursery followed in January 1923.[44] The Mexican Christian Institute was run by a core staff of four Anglo Disciples missionaries. In 1914 three of these, Dr. W. A. Alton, Mary Orvis, and Clara Hill, had first served in Mexico.[45] The missionaries were assisted by three "Mexican helpers," Manuel Lozano, José María Cueva, and Everardo Pérez.[46] In addition to the social services they offered, Sunday school and worship services were also held, though the formation of a second Mexican-Texan congregation was not an ultimate goal. Yet the social/cultural goals of the work of the Mexican Christian Institute to the Mexican-Texans were very clearly defined.

The purpose of this mission is to bring this large group of Mexican people—ignorant and superstitious and with a low standard of morals—

to a knowledge of Christ. . . . Why should we seek to bring Christ to the Spanish-speaking people in the United States? We are not only under obligation to our Lord to make Christians of these people, but we also have a *patriotic obligation* to make of them good citizens of our fair nation.[47]

Some examples of the articles which described the precarious financial situation of the Mexican pastors working in Texas have already been cited. In these can be found an unspoken reluctance to provide the resources needed for the success of these missions. Many of the articles described the needs of the different Mexican-Texan missions, needs such as adequate meeting space or an adequate salary for the pastor or for materials in Spanish. However, the fact that these needs are constantly reiterated is evidence that they mostly went unanswered. In contrast, the work done by the institute, which was under the direct supervision of Anglo missionaries assisted by "Mexican helpers," was always a popular cause within the denomination and was well supported in comparison to Mexican-Texan missions work. As a result, the Mexican Disciples Church, called the Laredo Street Mission, developed in the margins with little support from the Disciples. In 1914 Manuel Lozano, a Mexican Disciples who was already working at the institute with the missionaries, was also pastor of this small congregation.[48] Even after five years of continuous existence since its reorganization, the future of the mission at Laredo Street still seemed tenuous. This was how it was described in the November 1914 issue of *Missionary Tidings*:

> The work is here greatly hampered by the inadequate rented building even though it is much better than the one formerly occupied. The Roman Catholic church is near us in a magnificent pressed brick, the Baptist and Methodist churches occupy substantial buildings, while our work being carried on in an empty store room has no appearance of being permanent and gives us a poor standing at once with the better class of people.[49]

Despite the bleak report which describes the great unmet need of this mission for an adequate place to meet, it seems that Manuel Lozano's steadfastness paid off and the mission did not close its doors. Lozano, like all the other Mexican workers, is to be admired because, despite the many hardships he endured, he helped to keep alive this mission. The 1920–1921 *Year Book* reports a second reorganization of the Laredo Street Mission and lists the new membership at 42, with 17 additions, along with the name of the new pastor, Isaac Urango.[50] In that same year this congregation also purchased a lot with a small house on it for $1,400.[51] The house was used as a place for worship and was probably a tremendous improvement over the earlier facilities. A permanent church building for the Mexican Disciples Church was finally dedicated in September 1925, twenty-six years and two reorganizations after the mission was first started. The money to build the facilities, $24,292.21, came from the United Christian Missionary Society, which held the title to the property until the loan was repaid.[52] By the time the Mexican Disciples Church finally owned its building in 1925, its membership was at 150 and it was able to pay all its expenses "except the pastor's salary of $200 per month, which [was] paid by the United Christian Missionary Society."[53]

At the beginning of the second decade of the new century, the *Year Book* for 1921 reports only four Mexican-Texan churches still in existence. These were in San Antonio (pastor, Isaac Urango), Lockhart (pastor, Julian Salinas), Robstown (pastor, José Cueva) and a new church organized that same year in Tivoli.[54] This new start at Tivoli was visited once a month by Isaac Urango, pastor of the San Antonio church, and the following plea is made in the report: "This new work seems to be very promising. A pastor should be sent there as soon as possible. There is no other Protestant church working among the Mexicans in that part of the country."[55]

Despite the new church start in Tivoli, the fact that only four Mexican-Texan missions existed in 1921 meant that the Disciples had closed four earlier missions in El Paso, San Benito, Sabinal, and Martindale. If seven missions were begun in the period from 1899 to 1925, then the loss of four missions meant the Disciples had actually *decreased* their Mexican-Texan work by 58 percent during those first twenty-five years. The fact that there were established churches in only three Texas towns, San Antonio, Lockhart, and Robstown, did not provide much hope for the future of this missions work.

Second Phase of Work: 1926–1945

Churches Started: Amarillo (1926)
                      Mcallen (1927)
                      San Benito (Reorg. 1935)

The silence that surrounds the presence of the Mexican-Texan churches within the Disciples becomes more deafening throughout the twenty-nine years of the second phase of work. One of the first things I discovered in this research was how little was written about Disciples work with Mexican-Texans after the first phase of work. Not only is there little in print after 1925, but what did appear was not detailed and gave only brief information. The main sources for this section were the *Year Books* from 1925 to 1945, the short history written by Byron Spice in 1968, and a few other missionary newspapers. Another interesting discovery was that these sources often contradicted one another. It was only by a careful search through each year book that it was possible to create a clearer chronology. For example, the 1924 *Year Book* in the section on "The Spanish-American Work" mentions only the work of the Mexican Christian Institute and says nothing about the existing missions.[56] The next mention of Mexican-Texan missions work is found in the 1928 *Survey of Service*. In the chapter "Mexican Americans" there are only three churches listed as existing congregations, those in San Antonio, Robstown, and Lockhart.[57]

This information contradicts the information Byron Spice gives in his book. Spice says that during this time (1924–1928) churches in Amarillo and McAllen were organized. The church in Amarillo began in 1926 as a "project of both brotherhood [Disciples] and non-cooperative churches."[58] Perhaps the fact that the Amarillo mission was a joint project with other Protestant groups helps to explain why the UCMS does not claim it as a Disciples church start in its *Survey of Service* report. Fidel Reyes, the first Mexican-American Disciples to pastor in Texas, served in Amarillo from 1936 to 1947, and he was pastor when they built the church building, dedicated in June 1938.[59] This was a great achievement for the Amarillo congregation, which had been meeting in a "passenger train coach."[60] The *Survey of Service* also does not list the mission in McAllen, which Spice says was started in 1927 by "Pablo Gloria and the family of José Martinez."[61] In 1932 the McAllen church received help from the UCMS to build "a frame building." Despite their new simple church building, the church faced great economic hardships. Spice himself says that, "For years the congregation just barely survived."[62]

The 1935 *Year Book* lists Fred Vásquez as the pastor of the newly reorganized congregation in San Benito, This mission had been closed in 1916 as a result of the border disturbances caused by the Mexican Revolution. Vásquez's work in San Benito continued until 1939, when he moved to San Antonio to pastor the church there. The names of Pablo Gloria and Fred Vásquez are important to this period of history, because they were the first pastors of Disciples Mexican-Texan churches to attend and graduate from the Disciples university in Fort Worth, Texas Christian University.[63] Yet records are so meager in regard to Mexican-Texan work that Gloria and Vásquez are mentioned very briefly and only in Hall's history. Hall calls Gloria and Vásquez "Latin Americans," which most probably means that

Hall believed they were not born in Texas and were not Mexican-American, but this is not accurate.

Hall also does not give the actual dates of their attendance at TCU nor say when they graduated. However, *Year Book* information tells us that Pablo Gloria probably enrolled in TCU in the early to mid-1920s, because he is listed in 1924 as involved in a new Mexican-Texan mission in Fort Worth.[64] Fred Vásquez was probably enrolled in TCU in the early 1930s, because he is listed in the *Year Book* as already serving the reorganized congregation in San Benito from 1935 to 1939.

Other listings in the various *Year Books* tell us where in Texas other efforts were made to start Mexican-Texan churches throughout the 1930s. For example, there is only one mention made in 1930 of a new mission in Donna which was led by Garland H. Farmer, who eventually went to Puerto Rico as a missionary. In 1936 three missions were started. One was in Dallas, under the leadership of José P. García. A second one was in Marfa, where the name of Pablo Gloria appears as the first pastor in 1939. And the third one was opened in Sweetwater, though it was never assigned a pastor in the eighteen years it was listed in the year books. All three churches were eventually closed, the one in Dallas in 1949 or 1950, the one in Marfa in 1950 or 1951, and the one in Sweetwater in 1943. (The lack of source material makes the exact dates difficult to determine.)

And so, at the close of 1945, and after half a century of efforts to start churches among the Mexican-Texans, the Disciples had a total of seven established congregations, in Amarillo, Dallas, Lockhart, McAllen, Robstown, San Antonio, and San Benito. These are very discouraging numbers, but they are also crucial indicators of the tensions with which the Texas Disciples struggled. They tried to respond to the mandate to "go and preach," yet throughout their work they saw the Mexican-Texan people through the distorted lenses of the historical, cultural, racial, and social ethos of the Texas borderlands. The next section will review the development of this shortsighted approach to missions work with the Mexican-Texans.

Anglo Disciples In Texas

The Early Years: 1830–1840

The Disciples of Texas originally entered the borderlands of Coahuila y Texas as foreign settlers invited by the Mexican government. Soon after their arrival they joined the other North American settlers in support of the revolution, which led to the creation of the Republic of Texas and then to eventual annexation of Texas to the United States. The founding leaders of the Disciples of Christ were never outspoken pacifists during the years preceding the Mexican-American War, though they had expressed pacifist tendencies in their writings. Alexander Campbell had used the *Millennial Harbinger* [65] as the primary vehicle in which to share his views about war and peace with other Disciples. In fact, he dealt with the subject of war from the first issue of the *Christian Baptist* down to his last written comments in the *Millennial Harbinger* in the midst of the Civil War.[66] Campbell's writings from the 1830s show the influence of the American peace movement, which was organized in 1828, upon his thinking. However, when the war with Mexico broke out on May 13, 1846, Campbell was no longer faced with the idea of war in the abstract, but instead with the reality of war.

Campbell wrote an article which appeared in the November 1846 issue of the *Millennial Harbinger*, in which he continued to generally oppose war and used the Scripture as the basis for his principles.[67] In this article Campbell claims to have maintained his pacifist position. He wrote:

> While I must, for more reasons than one, decline the task of scrutinizing the existing war either in its object, character, or tendency, I feel it due to those claiming my views, to give them freely on the whole subject of war as compatible or incompatible with the genius of the Christian religion. . . . From this view of the subject my observations and reflections ever since, have subtracted nothing. On the contrary. . . . My convictions have rather become stronger than weaker.[68]

His primary reason for not dealing directly with the Mexican-American War was his desire to avoid sectional issues in the church which could lead to schism. However, the irony is that while Campbell seemed to voice the same attitude of peace he had advocated through the years, his ideas about the Mexican-American War were quite defined. He stated that his original convictions against war had only "become stronger," but then he makes a very revealing statement. Campbell wrote ". . . of the war in general, and of the present American Mexican Republican War in particular; a war *kindly* undertaken for the *benevolent* purpose of acquiring more territory, for the *improvement* of the condition of the African slaves, and for *civilizing* and *Christianizing* the priest ridden Mexican."[69] He may have been opposed to the abstract idea of war because it was against the "genius of Christianity," but he was quite transparent in his feelings about the actual war with Mexico.

The very telling declaration Campbell made in the November 1846 issue of the *Millennial Harbinger* fits the man, his theology, and his historical location. As a New Testament primitivist, Campbell found in the Bible no divinely revealed guidelines for political life. He held that political judgments made by the Christian were not faith issues, but solely "opinions" and were therefore to be treated as an individual matter. Campbell, as a Southerner, was also a moderate in regard to slavery. While he believed slavery was a great misfortune, he did not see it as a sin.[70] Again, this was reflected in his statement, but Campbell was also a product of the frontier, whose confidence in the United States and its promise was not easily shaken.

He believed in the predestination of the nation and in the flourishing of Protestantism, especially in the midst of "priest ridden Mexicans."[71] Campbell was also very clearly anti-Roman Catholic. In the August 1832 issue of the *Millennial Harbinger* he dealt with Roman Catholicism for the first time in print "when he reprinted a sketch of the history of the Jesuits 'taken from a late edition of Paschal's letters.'"[72] Harold Lunger writes that in November 1833 he launched

> a series of articles on the "Catholic Controversy," which he characterized as "one of the most important controversies of this controversial age," important in its bearings both upon religion and "upon the political destinies of this nation, involving the fundamental principles of free government." ... By 1835, when the religious leaders of [North] America were generally engaged in "saving the West from the Pope," Campbell began to reflect elements of the nativist argument.[73]

In October 1836 Campbell gave an address at the College of Teachers in Cincinnati entitled, "Importance of Uniting the Moral with the Intellectual Culture of the Mind."[74] In this address Campbell praised the cultural superiority of the English-speaking people, which he believed was due mainly to the Protestant Reformation. The Roman Catholic Bishop Purcell of Cincinnati took issue with Campbell's comments, and a debate was eventually held between the two men in January 1837. Campbell sought to defend seven propositions against Roman Catholicism, and in the last one he made this declaration: "The Roman Catholic religion, if infallible and unsusceptible of reformation, as alleged, is essentially anti-American, being opposed to the genius of all free institutions, and positively subversive to them."[75]

What we hear echoed in Campbell's words was the premise commonly held by the North American settlers who moved west: Protestantism stood for democracy and was intimately connected with the future and promise of the United States. The republican form of government, which the United States enjoyed, was the result of its direct link with Protestantism. Believing this to be so, which Campbell and many others did, they could then argue that Roman Catholicism was anti-American. Again, as with the slave issue and with his theological concerns, Campbell was speaking from within his historical and cultural location. The social issues of Campbell's historical location were also those of the entire United States in the mid-to-late nineteenth century. Slavery, manifest destiny, and a strong anti-Catholic sentiment became important influences in determining the attitudes of both the Disciples and of the nation in the mid-to-late nineteenth century.[76] That was why Campbell could not absolutely condemn the expansionist Mexican-American War. Campbell did indeed believe this war had a benevolent purpose and that its result would be to the benefit of two inferior races living in the United States. This war would ultimately "improve" the condition of the African slave and it would also "civilize and Christianize" the Mexican.

This same sentiment was also expressed by Robert Forrester, who was co-editor with Walter Scott of the *Protestant Unionist*. Also writing in November 1846, Forrester was not as diplomatic in his wording as Campbell had been. He wrote: "Popish intolerance standing opposed to the popular current of the age, if it refuse to yield, must be swept away by its overwhelming force."[77] The diverse opinions about the Mexican-American War proved that the Disciples were far from united in their ideas. But they also showed that as a religious body their theology reflected the values and concerns of their culture. While voices of protest against the war were raised, which triggered much debate on the subject, sectional interests based on geography were ultimately reflected in the positions taken by the various Disciples leaders and congregations. In addition, the strong anti-Catholic prejudice found in the United States, and shared by many Disciples, was an important ideological justification for the war. The fact that many of the Texas Disciples had been active in the Texas Revolution and had strong anti-Mexican sentiments only further guaranteed that the Disciples in Texas would support and fight in the Mexican-American War.[78]

Decades of Conflict: 1880–1900

The decades of the 1850s until 1900 were a time of great growth for the Disciples across the United States. From 1840 to 1850 the Disciples increased from 40,000 to 118,000; they increased from 118,000 to 225,000 from 1860 to 1870; and from 1874 to 1900 the national figures grew from 400,000 to 1,120,000.[79] However, in Texas the Disciples did not grow as quickly nor expand rapidly across the state. In 1860 they were still located mostly in the northeastern and central eastern part of the state. It was not until 1905 that the Disciples moved as far south as Corpus Christi. The first record of any Disciples in the Río Grande Valley was in the city of Brownsville and was dated 1907.[80] This was a relatively late start for Disciples missions work given the fact that the Methodists were already in Brownsville in 1849 and the first Protestant church to be organized in the Río Grande Valley was started in 1850, also in Brownsville, by the Presbyterians.[81] It took the Texas Disciples more than half a century to reach the Río Grande Valley where the majority of Mexican-Texans lived.

In an attempt to explain this late movement by the Disciples toward southern Texas and their very slow start in developing a ministry among Tejanos, the following significant factors can be suggested. (1) The Disciples movement experienced great internal dissension on a national level in the 1870s and 1880s, and in Texas in the 1880s and 1890s. This internal strife promoted an inward-looking protectionist attitude in the leaders and congregations that hindered the development of a broad and clearly defined missions theology. While the Disciples were known for their earlier tent-meetings and strong evangelistic focus, they did not keep up with or adequately respond to the changing demographics of the United States at the end of the nineteenth century. (2) The Disciples in Texas remained mainly a rural people who did not show much interest in missions work in the growing cities of Texas, nor in the immigrant groups in those cities or throughout the state. (3) The frontier ethos that shaped the Disciples in Texas also greatly influenced how they did their missions and how they perceived the population groups that were not Euro-American. Instead of reshaping or molding the frontier ideals of land, manifest destiny, and choseness to "the genius of Christianity," the Disciples uncritically incorporated them into their missions theology. As a result, the vision for missions of the Disciples in Texas was short-sighted and narrow. This is made evident by the lack of interest Disciples demonstrated toward non-Caucasian and non-Protestant groups. As a result and in comparison with the other Protestant denominations in Texas, the Disciples did minimal work with non-Anglo groups. A more detailed examination of these three factors will provide further insight.

After the death of Alexander Campbell in 1866, the Disciples movement as a whole entered a period of internal dissension. At the heart of the conflict was the tension between union and restoration, a tension whose seeds Campbell himself had unwittingly sown. During the early years of his leadership, called by some Disciples historians Campbell's years of "iconoclasm" (1823–1830), his overriding goal was restoration based on an almost literal interpretation of the Bible. Because of this, Campbell vigorously opposed the creation of any Christian organization not supported by Scripture. Campbell's ideal was the church as a "community of communities." However, as the Disciples movement continued to grow and expand, the need for polity became one of pressing importance.

Being pragmatic, Alexander Campbell accepted the need for internal organization, and in the 1840s his writings reflected his re-evaluation of his early restoration position.[82] In 1849 Campbell supported the creation of two key bodies. The first one was the General Convention of the Christian Churches, which in turn organized the American Christian Missionary Society. Campbell not only supported the creation of these two new nonscripturally supported organizations, but he served as the first president of the American Christian Missionary Society from 1849 until his death in 1866. Despite Campbell's support for the creation of these two bodies, many Disciples continued to consider them as nonscriptural and therefore out-of-step with the movement's original restoration ideal. However, while Campbell was alive and publicly supported the new societies, the denomination was able to maintain unity. But in the 1870s, after his death, strife within the Disciples could no longer be contained.

The most influential vehicle for the expression of the restoration ideal and opposition to innovation was the *Gospel Advocate*, first published in Nashville in 1855. Because the largest group of settlers in Texas was from Kentucky and Tennessee,[83] it is not surprising that a strong and vocal group of conservative Disciples formed the basis for the Christian Church in Texas. Open conflict among the Disciples in Texas began in 1880 at the state-meeting in Waxahachie. At this meeting the creation of an organization (society) was proposed that would provide cooperation for missions work among all Disciples congregations in Texas. It took six years of debate, conflict, and turmoil to reach a decision. In 1884 the creation of a conservative Disciple newspaper, *The Firm Foundation*, added its voice to the litany of dissension. In this new periodical the gospel of primitive Christianity, strongly undergirded by the preachers from Nashville, was disseminated in Texas,[84] but the time had come to finally take action.

In 1886, at the Disciples State Convention in Austin, a vote was taken to create a state missionary society to be called the Texas Christian Missionary Society. The result of the vote was a division which, because of the loose organization of the Disciples, was felt immediately in the local congregations as many withdrew their membership. But the situation would only worsen. The conflict over the missionary society was followed in the 1890s by other conflicts over the use of organ music in Disciples worship, open membership, creeds, and the paying of salaries to ministers.[85] During these difficult years churches in Dallas, Sherman, Paris, Fort Worth, McGregor, Waco, Denton, Hillsboro[86] and other cities were divided and many people left the Disciples. As a result, the Christian Church in Texas experienced a stagnation which affected the overall growth of the Disciples in Texas. Energies which could have been directed toward missions work were spent on internal dissension. This also meant that the Disciples were not equipped during the last two decades of the nineteenth century to deal with the Spanish-speaking Tejano population. Such work required of the Disciples a better organized and equipped missions effort than was yet in place. It also required a church that was stable enough to produce defined mission goals which would lead it to invest both energies and resources in its surrounding communities.

If the last two decades of the 1800s were a time of inner turmoil and division for the Texas Disciples, the fact that the Disciples were still very much a rural and frontier people did little to help them actively develop missions work among the large Tejano population in the state. Carter E. Boren writes in his history that this rural mindset was what prevented Disciples from developing an early and strong ministry in the growing cities of San Antonio and Houston.[87] The Disciples did not begin a church in San Antonio until 1889, again another late start, since by 1875 there were already six Protestant churches in that city.[88] Boren says, "The Disciples have never been quite able to overcome their initial aversion to cities."[89] This mindset is important to point out because it was reinforced by a frontier mentality that in its provincialism was not open to change. As a result, the understanding of the national mission (or homeland missions) of the Christian Church was adversely affected.

Conclusion

As the nineteenth century drew to an end, the Disciples found themselves struggling in the face of a a society that was strange and alien to them in many ways. Their early years as a frontier church in the southeastern states of the United States were successful ones. As the Disciples followed the frontier's expansion and moved to the southwestern borderlands, however, there were new and powerful forces that would shape their theology and identity. These forces, which have never been critically dealt with, had more to do with the political and economic ideologies that were shaping the frontier than with the the Gospel message. The Disciples, who claimed to be a people whose only compass was Scripture, now found themselves playing the role of colonizers. They faced the colonization of lands that brought them into contact with a government that was not only foreign because it was Mexican, but whose people were Roman Catholic mestizos whose language, race, religion, and culture were alien. As the Disciples took upon themselves the role of colonizers, their theological paradigms and their religious worldview were exposed to the very strong and influential forces external to the Bible; forces created by the economic, political, and social concerns of the Euro-Americans who had entered the Mexican borderlands. These forces successfully combined theological concepts with ideologies of conquest, such as destined use of the land or the self-identificaton as a chosen people, which became rationalizations for creating racial paradigms of inferiority and Other-ness. These ideologies were not created by Disciples but were the product of many other forces, such as slavery and the economic interests of an expanding capitalist economy, and they permeated the nineteenth-century expansionism that had become so important for the United States as a political and military entity. The influence and power of these ideologies cannot be underestimated nor dismissed—neither in their capacity to shape the U.S. political agenda toward the southwestern borderlands nor in their capacity to shape Protestantism.

Perhaps the Disciples did not in a conscious or deliberate way begin to absorb and be absorbed by these influences, but there is historical evidence that they were not exempt from them. So it happened that the religion of the colonizers merged with concerns for domination of the land, with self-determination, with economic domination; and in this process, the theology and theological identity of the Disciples would forever be altered. If we add to this the internal strife and divisions that the Disciples as a denomination began to experience in the late-1800s, we further understand why they were not able to more critically examine and refute such external forces. The powerful effects of these influences were distinctly manifested in how the Disciples related to the people and cultures that were unlike their own not in the overseas missions field, but right *in* the United States. The sad irony is that history shows that the Disciples had been active missionaries *outside* their national borders since 1851.[1] However *within* their national borders, the Disciples had not been able to develop an encompassing theology of homeland missions that reaches out to other races, nationalities, and cultures. As the United States received a great influx of immigrants in the late 1800s and into the 1900s, the Disciples had little in common with the newly arriving Roman Catholic Italian and Irish immigrants. This was mostly due to their English and Scottish heritage, which was markedly anti-Catholic. They also did not appeal to the Germans, who were mostly Lutherans or Reformed.[2] They did not focus their national missions work on the cities, so they did little with the urban poor and did not address the social issues facing the growing cities.

In the Texas borderlands in particular, even though the Disciples lived in close proximity to millions of Mexican-Texans, these Others, "strangers," remained either invisible or simply nonexistent to them. The obvious neglect of the Tejanos in the Disciples missions work is the result, in part, of the very powerful external factors already discussed. However, there is still one more crucial force that must be mentioned: Texas Disciples were also shaped by the powerful frontier ethos itself. It was this ethos that helped to produce a Protestant denomination that valued and sought to preserve "the Christian freedom that is found in the New Testament, the natural rights of man, and the democratic society of which [the Disciples] formed a part."[3] It was an

ethos that facilitated the melding of Protestantism with the ideologies
of manifest destiny and patriotism, divine chosenness and capitalist
economic interests. It was an ethos that racialized the Texas borderlands, which in turn led to the displacement of the original landowners who happened to be non-Caucasian. It was an ethos that made the
North American God a Protestant, one who had little patience for the
superstition and ignorance promoted by Roman Catholicism. Perhaps
we can better understand why the Texas Disciples moved so slowly
into the southern part of the state.

When Disciples historian Carter E. Boren tries to give an explanation
for this slow advance into the Río Grande Valley, he arrives at two reasons. First, he states the obvious demographic fact that North-Central
Texas was the center of Euro-American population for the state, so this
part of Texas was the most likely place for Disciples to stay. But he also
makes the following observation: "Two factors have mainly deterred the
Disciple church developing [in the southern part of the state]: namely,
(1) the area, especially in the lower Río Grande Valley, was still populated with inhabitants of Mexican extraction at the beginning of the century, and (2) the territory is a twentieth-century development."[4]

What Boren is pointing out are two very distinct factors, or realities.
Who the inhabitants of South Texas were is crucial to this analysis because it has to do with how Disciples perceived the Tejanos. Given the
prevalence of anti-Catholic sentiments before the Mexican-American
War, as well as the continued development of distinct racial catego-
ries for the Tejanos after the Texas Revolution of 1836, it is not surprising that Texas Disciples would uncritically perceive and therefore
treat the Tejano as truly Other. The second reason Boren gives for the
absence of the Disciple church in the south is that the territory was
undeveloped. Irrigation practices were not fully developed until 1900.
Boren's second reason raises the issue of land use and development
and of the economics of race—who had ownership and control of the
land—which ultimately led to the displacement of the Tejano as land-
owner.[5] Again we find how the land itself is an influence on the missions theology of Protestant denominations.

The Texas Disciples shared with the other North American settlers
the surety that they were *the* new heirs to the promise of Texas. The
Mexican-Texan was not only of another race (or mixture of races, which
was worse), but also Roman Catholic. Given these characteristics, the
North American settlers perceived the *Tejanos* as inferior in many
ways. And it was accepted by the dominant group that it was because
the Mexican-Texan possessed these inherent flaws that they had been
supplanted by a "new" people who now would dominate borderlands

history. The Mexican-Texan therefore became the displaced Other, strangers in their own land, not landowners but renters or squatters.

Boren concludes his examination of the work of Disciples with Mexican-Texans by making the following insightful statement:

> Indifference and racial prejudice largely characterized the relationship of the Texas Disciples toward opportunities for service among both Negroes and Mexicans. The size of these racial elements in the state, especially in regard to Mexicans, and their limited economic and social status, have offered unusual opportunities for an extensive program of service that has been neglected.[6]

The Disciples may have learned how to articulate a theology of homeland missions that claimed to be inclusive and colorblind, but the history of what they actually did in Texas, where they were surrounded for over a century by a large and accessible Mexican-Texan population, tells another story. The "do as you go" paradigm became the fundamental operating method for the ministry of Texas Disciples in the Mexican-Texan communities. No resources were invested in educating and developing indigenous leaders; no resources were invested in printing materials in Spanish; local missions were underfunded and neglected; the Mexican leader was seen as a "helper" and not given equal status. And, as a result, the Disciples church in Texas created a Latino church that was relegated to the margins of the denomination's focus and resources. In these early years of work, the Texas Disciples also helped to give shape to the the patterns of acceptance and support for future work among Latinos.

If a Mexican-Texan Disciples mission succeeded, God was praised and the missionary society had pictures taken to assist with future fundraising efforts (today it is done through videos). If it failed, the blame was placed on a people who made the work that much more difficult because they were "ignorant, irresponsible, roving and superstitious." And so, while the history of the Mexican-Texan Disciples churches can be said to be a history of neglect and marginality, this history is also a witness to the faith and perseverance of those early Latino leaders and their laity. It is a witness to their faith in the Gospel message, it is a witness to their untiring work, and a witness to their unwavering vision of a loving and inclusive God. These Mexican-Texan church leaders responded to their ministerial call and sought to serve their communities and to obey God, and did so with a selfless spirit and an unwavering belief in the universal Church of Jesus the Christ.

Notes

1. *The Design for the Christian Church (Disciples of Christ)*. Adopted by the General Assembly in 1968 and published annually in *The Yearbook for the Christian Church*.

Chapter One

1. Gilberto Hinojosa, "The Enduring Hispanic Faith Communities: Spanish and Texas Church Historiography," *The Journal of Texas Catholic History and Culture* 22 (March 1990): 20.

2. In order to clarify my naming of the frontier people who came from the United States into Spanish-Mexico Texas, I use the name "North America" to refer to the United States of America and "Euro-American" or "North American" to refer to citizens of the United States who moved westward. I believe the use of the term "American" to refer only to people from the United States is too narrow, and shows a certain arrogance, since "American" is also the correct way to refer to the Native People, Central Americans, and Latin Americans who are inhabitants of the Western Hemisphere. I use the term "Euro-American" to acknowledge that the Europeans who came to the United States came from all over Europe and not only from England.

3. I'd like to remind the reader that the reference in this section to the area called Texas does not refer to what is today the geographical state of Texas in the United States of America. The province of Texas, which was also called *Nueva Filipinas*, was quite small, or about one-half the size of the actual state. To talk about the Texas borderlands means to also include the colonial prov-

ince of Coahuila, which was to the south and west of Texas, much larger than Texas, and had its own provincial capital at Saltillo. To talk about the Texas borderlands means to also talk about the borderlands people. For more sources dealing with the "people already there," see Arnoldo De León, *The Tejano Community, 1836–1900* (Dallas, Tex.: Southern Methodist University Press, 1997), chap. 1; Oakah L. Jones, Jr., *Los Paisanos: Spanish Settlers on the Northern Frontier of New Spain* (Norman: University of Oklahoma Press, 1979); Gerald E. Poyo and Gilberto M. Hinojosa, eds., *Tejano Origins in Eighteenth-Century San Antonio* (Austin: University of Texas Press, 1991).

4. I use Hispanic and Latino interchangeably as terms broad enough to describe those people living in Texas (and the United States) who are Mexican-American and U.S. citizens, as well as those who have migrated from Mexico, the Spanish-speaking Caribbean, Central America, and South America.

5. Donald E. Worcester, "The Significance of the Spanish Borderlands to the United States," in *New Spain's Far Northern Frontier*, ed. David J. Weber (Albuquerque: University of New Mexico Press, 1979), 3.

6. T. R. Fehrenbach, *Lone Star: A History of Texas and the Texans* (New York: Macmillan, 1968), 78.

7. For a discussion of how "the coming of White people" has shaped the understanding of the history of Latin America, see Olivia Harris, "The Coming of White People: Reflections on the Mythologization of History in Latin America," *Bulletin of Latin American Research* 14, no. 1 (1995): 9–24.

8. Albert K. Weinberg, *Manifest Destiny: A Study of Nationalist Expansionism in American History* (Gloucester, Mass.: Peter Smith, 1958), 27.

9. Weinberg, *Manifest Destiny*, 43.

10. David J. Weber, *The Spanish Frontier in North America* (New Haven, Conn.: Yale University Press, 1992), 289.

11. Weber, *The Spanish Frontier in North America*, 290.

12. Weinberg, *Manifest Destiny*, 2.

13. Weber, *The Spanish Frontier in North America*, 272.

14. Ibid., 274.

15. Ibid.

16. Ibid.

17. Ibid.

18. Ibid., 282–283.

19. Ibid., 284.

20. Ibid., 292.

21. Ibid., 295.

22. Ibid., 292.

23. Ibid., 295.

24. Ibid., 297.

25. Frederick Merk, *Manifest Destiny and Mission in American History* (New York: Alfred A. Knopf, 1963), 7.

26. Ibid.

27. For an analysis of what the North American press said about the expansionism and filibustering taking place in Nueva España, see José Fuentes Mares, *Génesis del expansionismo norteamericano* (México, D.F: El Colegio de México, 1980), 58–67.

28. Ibid., 59.

29. Weber, *The Spanish Frontier*, 299, and Fuentes Mares, *Génesis del expansionismo*, 59.

30. Weber, *The Spanish Frontier*, 299.

31. Fuentes Mares, *Génesis del expansionismo*, 59–60. My translations unless otherwise noted.

32. Ibid., 60.

33. Weber, *The Spanish Frontier*, 295.

34. Ibid., 299.

35. Herbert I. Priestly, *The Mexican Nation: A History* (New York: Macmillan, 1938), 234.

36. Weber, *The Spanish Frontier*, 299.

37. Merk, *Manifest Destiny and Mission*, 8.

38. Ibid., 16.

39. Weinberg, *Manifest Destiny*, 55.

40. Merk, *Manifest Destiny and Mission*, 19–20.

41. Ibid., 20.

42. Weber, *The Spanish Frontier*, 300.

43. Herbert E. Bolton, *Wider Horizons of American History* (New York: D. Appleton Century, Inc., 1939), 52.

44. David J. Weber, *The Mexican Frontier, 1821–1846* (Albuquerque: University of New Mexico Press, 1982), 277.

45. Bolton, *Wider Horizons*, 72.

46. For an in-depth analysis of the *Tejano* culture that existed in the Texas borderlands when the first Euro-American settlers arrived in the early nineteenth century, see Arnoldo de León, *The Tejano Community, 1836–1900* (Dallas: Southern Methodist University Press, 1997).

47. Arnoldo De León, *They Called Them Greasers: Anglo Attitudes towards Mexicans in Texas, 1821–1900* (Austin: University of Texas Press, 1983), 1.

48. See Weinberg, *Manifest Destiny*, 72–99.

49. Ibid., 74–75.

50. See Reginald Horsman, *Race and Manifest Destiny: The Origins of Racial Anglo-Saxonism* (Cambridge, Mass.: Harvard University Press, 1981), for a detailed analysis of the development of the idea of Anglo-Saxon superiority, especially after the 1850s.

51. An early example of this emphasis on "right doctrine" (orthodoxy) by the Disciples mission workers can be found in *Missionary Tidings* 6, no. 6 (October 1888): 8–9.

52. Weinberg, *Manifest Destiny*, 8.

53. Ibid., 17.

54. Ibid.

55. Compare Horsman's *Race and Manifest Destiny* and De León's *They Called Them Greasers*. While both historians trace the development of the ideas of racial superiority and how these racial attitudes influenced both the politics and the culture of the time, they argue that these attitudes appeared in different periods in U.S. history. Horsman holds that it was in the mid-1800s and into the early 1900s that these "rampant doctrines" really flourished. De León argues that in the case of Texas, Euro-American settlers' attitudes of racial superiority were already present in that first encounter of the Austin colonizers with the indigenous Texans in 1821. De León is critical of the Texas historians who have continuously overlooked "a long racist and ethnocentric tradition towards blacks and Indians that was transposed upon native Texas castas as a matter of course" (x). For those interested in a historical tracing of "Hispanophobic" attitudes all the way to the sixteenth century, see Philip Wayne Powell, *Tree of Hate: Propaganda and Prejudices Affecting United States Relations with the Hispanic World* (New York: Basic Books, 1971).

56. De León, *They Called Them Greasers*, 3.

57. The Spaniards were, of course, not the first people to live in the Texas borderlands. For an examination of the interaction between the Spanish and the Native People who lived in Texas, see William B. Gannett, *The American Invasion of Texas, 1820–1845: Patterns of Conflict Between Settlers and Indians* (Ph.D. diss., Cornell University, 1990). For an examination of the interaction between North Americans and Native populations, see Richard Drinnon, *Facing West: The Metaphysics of Indian-Hating and Empire Building* (Minneapolis: University of Minnesota Press, 1980).

58. Gerald E. Poyo and Gilberto M. Hinojosa, "Spanish Texas and Borderlands Historiography in Transition: Implications for United States History," *The Journal of American History* 75 (September 1988): 403.

59. It would be most interesting to hear what our present-day politicians and immigration policy makers have to say about these nineteenth-century North American "wetbacks."

60. Weber, *The Mexican Frontier, 1821–1846*, 278.

61. Poyo and Hinojosa, "Spanish Texas," 394.

62. Weber, *The Mexican Frontier, 1821–1846*, 277.

63. Ibid., 278.

64. Poyo and Hinojosa, 410, n. 28.

65. Ibid., 411.

66. Weber, *The Spanish Frontier*, 308.

67. Weber, *The Mexican Frontier, 1821–1846*, 278.

68. Oakah L. Jones, Jr., *Los Paisanos: Spanish Settlers on the Northern Frontier of New Spain* (Norman: University of Oklahoma Press, 1979), 53.

69. Jones, *Los Paisanos*, 53–54.

70. Arnoldo De León, *Mexican Americans in Texas: A Brief History* (Arlington Heights, Ill: Harlan Davidson, 1993), 12.

71. Ibid., 12.

72. Jones, *Los Paisanos*, 54.
73. Poyo and Hinojosa, "Spanish Texas," 406.
74. Ibid., 407.
75. Ibid.
76. Ibid., 406, n. 23.
77. De León, *Mexican Americans in Texas*, 19.
78. De León, *The Tejano Community, 1836–1900*, 3.
79. De León, *Mexican Americans in Texas*, 20.
80. Ibid., 23.

Chapter Two

1. Winfred E. Garrison, *Religion Follows the Frontier* (New York: Harper & Brothers Publishers, 1931), 199–200.
2. Frederick Jackson Turner (1861–1932), United States historian, professor at the University of Wisconsin and Harvard University. For a brief biography and analysis of Jackson's thesis, see James D. Bennett, *Frederick Jackson Turner* (Boston, Mass.: Twayne Publishers, 1975).
3. This meeting was held in conjunction with the World's Columbian Exposition, which was a belated commemoration of Columbus's voyage to the Americas. Turner's paper was first published in the *Proceedings of the State Historical Society of Wisconsin*, December 14, 1893.
4. Bennett, *Frederick Jackson Turner*, 36.
5. Ibid., 41.
6. Ibid., 39.
7. Ibid., 41–42.
8. Ibid.
9. David W. Noble, *Historians Against History* (Minneapolis: University of Minnesota Press, 1965), 23–24.
10. Roderick Nash, *Wilderness and the American Mind*, 3d. ed. (New Haven, Conn.: Yale University Press, 1982), 149.
11. The term "man" or "men" will be used throughout this chapter to refer to the generic person/human. I do this because the writers whose ideas I am discussing take it for granted that men are the representatives of their species and not women. To use the contemporary "he or she" would not be in keeping with the authentic historical voice of these writers.
12. Frederick Jackson Turner, *The Significance of the Frontier in American History* (State Historical Society of Wisconsin,1893; reprint, El Paso: Academic Reprints, 1960), 24.
13. Jackson K. Putnam, "The Turner Thesis and the Westward Movement: A Reappraisal," *Western Historical Quarterly* 7 (October 1976): 381.
14. Turner, *The Significance of the Frontier in American History*, 1.
15. Putnam, "The Turner Thesis," 378.
16. Turner, *The Significance of the Frontier in American History*, 2.

17. Ibid., 4.

18. Ibid.

19. Ibid., 6.

20. Ibid., 14–17.

21. Turner, *The Significance of the Frontier in American History*, 17.

22. Ibid., 28.

23. Ibid., 29.

24. For some good examples of this literature, see Merrill E. Lewis, "The Art of Frederick Jackson Turner," *Wisconsin Academy of Sciences, Arts and Letters, Transactions* 59 (1971): 23–32; and in the same journal, Ray A. Billington, "Frederick Jackson Turner, Non-Western Historian," 7–21. For a survey of the Turner and anti-Turner debate, see Ray A. Billington, *The American Frontier Thesis: Attack and Defense* (Washington, D.C.: American Historical Association, 1971). See also Lee Benson, "The Historian as Mythmaker: Turner and the Closed Frontier," in David M. Ellis, ed., *The Frontier in American Development: Essays in Honor of Paul Wallace Gates* (Ithaca, N.Y.: University of Cornell Press, 1969), 3–19; and Noble, *Historians Against History*.

25. Turner, *The Significance of the Frontier in American History*, 29.

26. Noble, *Historians Against History*, 38.

27. Turner, *The Significance of the Frontier in American History*, 9.

28. Noble, *Historians Against History*, 38.

29. Putnam, "The Turner Thesis" 382.

30. Nash, *Wilderness and the American Mind*, 144.

31. Roderick Nash discusses this feeling of loss in the United States as the country became more and more urban and industrial in his chapter "The Wilderness Cult," ibid., 141–160.

32. Ibid., 142.

33. See note 31.

34. Nash, *Wilderness and the American Mind*, 146.

35. Ibid., 147.

36. Putnam, "The Turner Thesis, 390.

37. Ibid., 398.

38. Ibid., 403.

39. Myra Jehlen, *American Incarnation* (Cambridge: Harvard University Press, 1986), 2.

40. Ibid., 3.

41. Putnam, "The Turner Thesis," 386.

42. Frederick Jackson Turner, "The Problem of the West," in *Frontier and Section: Selected Essays of Frederick Jackson Turner*, with an introduction by Ray Allen Billington (Englewood Cliffs, N.J.: Prentice-Hall, 1961), 70.

43. Jehlen, *American Incarnation*, 25.

44. Turner, *The Significance of the Frontier in American History*, 2.

45. Ibid., 3.

46. Turner, *The Problem of the West*, 68.

47. Turner, *The Significance of the Frontier in American History*, 23.

48. Turner, *The Problem of the West*, 68.

49. Putnam, "The Turner Thesis," 387.

50. Jehlen, 29 "American Incarnation," [emphasis mine].

51. Turner, *The Significance of the Frontier in American History*, 2.

52. Turner's focus when talking about the "savage" who encounters the pioneer is specifically on the Native American population in Michigan, Ohio, Iowa, Illinois, and Florida. He makes no mention, nor does he show any awareness of the Mexican population in the southwestern United States, which the frontier people also encountered as early as the 1820s.

53. Turner, *The Problem of the West*, 69.

54. Nash, *Wilderness and the American Mind*, 152–153.

55. Forrest G. Wood, *The Arrogance of Faith* (New York: Alfred A. Knopf, 1990), 217.

56. Ibid., 210.

57. Robert Jewett, *The Captain America Complex* (Philadelphia: Westminster Press, 1973), 9.

58. Turner, *The Significance of the Frontier in American History*, 12.

59. Ibid., 11.

60. Reginald Horsman, *Race and Manifest Destiny* (Cambridge, Mass.: Harvard University Press, 1981), 190.

61. Turner, *The Significance of the Frontier in American History*, 10.

62. Ibid.

63. Horsman, *Race and Manifest Destiny*, 190.

64. Ibid.

65. Albert K. Weinberg, *Manifest Destiny: A Study of Nationalist Expansionism in American History* (Gloucester: Peter Smith, 1958), 162.

66. Turner, *The Problem of the West*, 69–70.

67. Wood, *Arrogance of Faith*, 213–214.

68. Ibid., 213.

69. Thomas R. Hietala, *Manifest Destiny: Anxious Aggrandizement in Late Jacksonian America* (Ithaca, N.Y.: Cornell University Press, 1985), 132.

70. Ibid., 4.

71. Wood, *Arrogance of Faith*, 214.

72. Hietala, *Manifest Destiny*, 132.

73. Weinberg, *Manifest Destiny: A Study*, 83.

74. Horsman, *Race and Manifest Destiny*, 193.

75. Nott was also involved in the English translation of *Essai sur l'inégalité des races humaines* (1853–1855), written by Comte Joseph Arthur de Gobineau, a work "considered by many European and American scholars to be the most authoritative statement on 'Aryan superiority and racial determinism'" (Wood, 214).

76. Wood, *Arrogance of Faith*, 215.

77. Ibid., 220–221.

78. Ibid., 223.

79. Putnam, "The Turner Thesis," 379.

80. Reginald Horsman provides a good examination of the dissemination of what he calls "scientific racialism" in Chapter 8, 139–158, of *Race and Manifest Destiny*.

81. Ibid., 139, 142.

82. Ibid., 143.

83. Ibid., 143.

84. Ibid., 145.

85. Ibid., 156–157 [emphasis mine].

86. Ibid., 191.

87. De León, *They Called Them Greasers*, 2.

88. Ibid., 6.

89. Ibid., 4.

90. Ibid., 7.

91. Ibid., 9.

92. Weinberg, *Manifest Destiny: A Study*, 163.

93. Horsman, *Race and Manifest Destiny*, 210.

Chapter Three

1. The present name Christian Church (Disciples of Christ) appealed to its founders who sought the ideal of unity in the Christian body. Yet the name preferred by Alexander Campbell, one of its founders, and the one commonly used to refer to members of this denomination or used by members to refer to themselves is "Disciples" or "Disciples of Christ," or even "Restorationists." The form Christian Church (Disciples of Christ) did not come into official use until 1968.

2. George E. Beazley, Jr., "Who Are the Disciples?" in *The Christian Church (Disciples of Christ): An Interpretative Examination in the Cultural Context*, ed. George E. Beazley, Jr. (St. Louis, Mo.: The Bethany Press, 1973), 6.

3. This introductory chapter will provide only a brief survey of the early history of the Christian Church (Disciples of Christ). For a more complete history of this early period, see W. E. Garrison, *Religion Follows the Frontier* (New York: Harper & Brothers, 1931); W. E. Garrison and A.T. DeGroot, *The Disciples of Christ: A History* (St. Louis, Mo.: The Bethany Press, 1948); Lester McAllister and William E. Tucker, *Journey in Faith: A History of the Christian Church (Disciples of Christ)* (St. Louis, Mo.: The Bethany Press, 1975).

4. Beazley, *The Christian Church*, 21.

5. Garrison, *Religion Follows the Frontier*, 3.

6. Ibid.

7. Beazley, *The Christian Church*, 21.

8. Kenneth Teegarden, *We Call Ourselves Disciples* (St. Louis, Mo.: The Bethany Press, 1975), 16.

9. Garrison, *Religion Follows the Frontier*, 98.

10. Ibid., 98–99.

11. Ibid., 99.

12. Ibid., 101.

13. Ibid., 102.

14. Ibid., 103.

15. Ibid., 104.

16. Ibid.

17. Ibid.

18. Ibid., 117.

19. Ibid., 119.

20. Beazley, *The Christian Church*, 24.

21. Ronald E. Osborn, "Theology Among Disciples," in *The Christian Church (Disciples of Christ): An Interpretative Examination in the Cultural Context*, ed. George E. Beazley, Jr. (St. Louis, Mo.: The Bethany Press, 1973), 86.

22. Garrison, *Religion Follows the Frontier*, 119.

23. Ibid., 127.

24. Ibid., 137.

25. Ibid., 64.

26. Beazley, *The Christian Church*, 21.

27. Garrison, *Religion Follows the Frontier*, 65.

28. Ibid., 67.

29. Ibid.

30. Ibid., 150.

31. Teegarden, *We Call Ourselves Disciples*, 18.

32. Various writers on the Disciples have developed a periodization to trace the movement's development. For an example of two periodizations that focus on the development of the Disciples' theology please see Ronald E. Osborn, "Theology Among Disciples" in *The Christian Church (Disciples of Christ): An Interpretive Examination in the Cultural Context*, ed. George E. Beazley (St. Louis, Mo.: The Bethany Press, 1975), 81–115; M. Eugene Boring, "The Disciples and Higher Criticism: The Crucial Third Generation," in *A Case Study of Mainstream Protestantism*, ed. D. Newell Willams (Grand Rapids, Mich.: Eerdmans, 1991), 29–70.

33. Garrison provides the following figures on the growth of the Disciples movement: "By 1850 the number had grown to 118,000—an almost threefold increase in a decade. . . . The next decade, 1850–1860, saw the numbers nearly doubled (225,000) and for 1870 the figure may be put, with fair accuracy, at 350,000" (p. 200). Ronald E. Osborn's figures of 225,000 Disciples in 1860 (p. 93) support Garrison's demographics. For information on later growth patterns, in the 1890s and beyond, see Roger W. Stump, "Spatial Patterns of Growth and Decline among the Disciples of Christ, 1890–1980" in *A Case Study of Mainstream Protestantism*, ed. D. Newell Willams (Grand Rapids, Mich.: Eerdmans, 1991), 445–468.

34. Garrison, *Religion Follows the Frontier*, 156.

35. Ibid., 157.

36. McAllister and Tucker, *Journey in Faith*, 145.

37. Garrison, *Religion Follows the Frontier*, 140.

38. Beazley, *The Christian Church*, 90.

39. Garrison, *Religion Follows the Frontier*, 146.

40. Ibid., 160.

41. Ibid., 11.

42. Alexander Campbell, *The Christian System in Reference to the Union of Christians and Restoration of Primitive Christianity as Plead by the Current Reformation* (Pittsburgh, Pa.: Forrester & Campbell, 1839), 12.

43. Beazley, *The Christian Church*, 88.

44. Ibid.

45. Ibid., 89.

46. Harold L. Lunger, *The Political Ethics of Alexander Campbell* (St. Louis, Mo.: The Bethany Press, 1954), 27.

47. Alexander Campbell, "Address on the Importance of Uniting the Moral with the Intellectual Culture of the Mind," in *Popular Lectures and Addresses* (Cincinnati, Ohio: Central Book Concern, 1879), 453. [Hereafter listed as *PLA*.]

48. Mark G. Toulouse, *Joined in Discipleship, the Maturing of an American Religious Movement* (St. Louis, Mo.: Chalice Press, 1992), 60.

49. See Garrison, *Religion Follows the Frontier,* 40–41, and Toulouse, *Joined in Discipleship,* 63–71. For an examination of the Churches of Christ, which trace their roots to the Stone-Campbell restorationist movement, see Bill J. Humble, "The Restorationist Ideal in the Churches of Christ," in Richard T. Hughes, ed., *The American Quest for the Primitive Church* (Urbana: University of Illinois Press, 1988), 220–231. In this essay Humble traces the restorationist theology of Thomas and Alexander Campbell between 1800 and 1850.

50. Toulouse, *Joined in Discipleship*, 64.

51. Garrison, *Religion Follows the Frontier*, 41.

52. Lunger, *Political Ethics*, 22.

53. Ibid., 17.

54. Ibid., 17–18.

55. Robert F. West, *Alexander Campbell and Natural Religion* (New Haven, Conn.: Yale University Press, 1948), 47.

56. Ibid., 48–49.

57. Ibid., 59.

58. Ibid.

59. Lunger, *Political Ethics*, 28.

60. Ibid., 34.

61. W. Clark Gilpin, "Faith on the Frontier: Historical Interpretations of the Disciples of Christ," in *A Case Study of Mainstream Protestantism*, ed. D. Newell Williams (Grand Rapids, Mich.: Eerdmans, 1991), 266.

62. Sydney Ahlstrom, *A Religious History of the American People* (New Haven, Conn.: Yale University Press, 1972), 451–452.

63. Richard T. Hughes, "From Primitive Church to Civil Religion: The

Millennial Odyssey of Alexander Campbell," *American Academy of Religion Journal* 44 (March 1976): 87.

64. Richard T. Hughes argues that after 1830 Alexander Campbell's thinking demonstrated an important shift from that of a "radical restorationist" to a more relaxed position, a change that had to do with "his recognition of a common religion [that secured] liberty, unity, and pluralism to an ultimate degree." Hughes, "From Primitive Church to Civil Religion: The Millennial Odyssey of Alexander Campbell," 96–101.

65. Donald G. Jones and Russell E. Richey, "The Civil Religion Debate," in *American Civil Religion*, ed. Jones and Richey (New York: Harper & Row, 1974), 15.

66. Hughes, "From Primitive Church," 89.

67. Lunger, *Political Ethics*, 67.

68. Ibid., 125.

69. Ibid., 131.

70. Ibid., 135.

71. Robert Jewett, *The Captain America Complex: The Dilemma of Zealous Nationalism* (Philadelphia, Pa.: Westminster Press, 1973), 31.

72. West, *Alexander Campbell*, 163.

73. Ibid., 164.

74. Ibid., 165.

75. See Alexander Campbell, "The Anglo-Saxon Language—Its Origin, Character, and Destiny," in *PLA,* 17–46.

76. Ibid., 31.

77. Ibid., 32.

78. Ibid., 40, 41, 44.

79. See Campbell, "The Destiny of our Country," in *PLA*, 162–185.

80. Ibid., 179.

81. Ibid., 184.

82. Ibid., 185.

83. W. E. Garrison does not see Campbell's millennial preoccupations as indicative that he had "any special interest in the second coming of Christ in a spectacular way or any marked devotion to either the premillennial or the postmillennial view. Apparently he used the term in quite a loose and general sense" (*Religions Follows the Frontier*, 147).

84. West, *Alexander Campbell*, 185.

85. Ibid., 217.

Chapter Four

1. Oakah L. Jones, Jr., *Los Paisanos, Spanish Settlers on the Northern Frontier of New Spain* (Norman: University of Oklahoma Press, 1979), 39.

2. David Weber, *The Spanish Frontier in North America* (New Haven, Conn.: Yale University Press, 1992), 153.

3. Weber, *Spanish Frontier*, 153.

4. William B. Gannett, *The American Invasion of Texas, 1820–1845: Patterns of Conflict between Settlers and Indians* (Ph.D. diss., Cornell University, 1984), 6.

5. Weber, *Spanish Frontier*, 306.

6. Ibid.

7. Ibid., 307.

8. Jones, *Los Paisanos*, 38.

9. Weber, *Spanish Frontier*, 163.

10. Jones, *Los Paisanos*, 41.

11. Gerald E. Poyo and Gilberto M. Hinojosa, "Spanish Texas and Borderlands Historiography in Transition: Implications for United States History," *The Journal of American History* 75 (September 1988): 399.

12. Arnoldo De León, *Mexican Americans in Texas: A Brief History* (Arlington Heights, Ill.: Harlan Davidson, 1993), 19.

13. Ibid., 21.

14. Ibid.

15. Ibid., 22.

16. Ibid.

17. Ibid., 23.

18. Nettie Lee Benson, "Texas as Viewed from Mexico, 1820–1834," *Southwestern Historical Quarterly* 90 (January 1987): 224–225.

19. Ibid., 225.

20. Ibid., 235–236.

21. William Stuart Red, *The Texas Colonists and Religion, 1821–1836* (Austin, Tex.: E. L. Shettles, 1924), 4. [Emphasis mine.]

22. Ibid., 3.

23. Joseph W. McKnight, "Stephen Austin's Legalistic Concerns," *Southwestern Historical Quarterly* 89 (January 1986): 240.

24. Howard Miller, "Stephen F. Austin and the Anglo-Texan Response to the Religious Establishment in Mexico, 1821–1836," *Southwestern Historical Quarterly* 91 (January 1988): 289.

25. Ibid., 290.

26. Ibid., 291.

27. Ibid., 293.

28. Henry Stuart Foote, *Texas and the Texans* (Philadelphia, Pa.: Thomas, Cowperthwait & Co., 1841; reprint, Austin: The Steck Co., 1935), 221.

29. W. R. Estep, "Religion in the Lone Star State: An Historical Perspective," *International Review of Mission* 78 (April 1989): 180.

30. Herbert I. Priestly, *The Mexican Nation, A History* (New York: Macmillan, 1938), 279.

31. McKnight, "Austin's Legalistic Concerns," 246.

32. David J. Weber, *Myth and the History of the Hispanic Southwest* (Albuquerque: University of New Mexico Press, 1988), 135.

33. Red, *The Texas Colonists*, 24.

34. Ibid., 25.
35. Miller, "Austin and the Anglo-Texan Response," 295–296.
36. Red, *The Texas Colonists*, 1.
37. Foote, *Texas*, 223.
38. Red, *The Texas Colonists*, 25.
39. Foote, *Texas*, 223. This same law also gave Mexican citizens the right to buy up to 11 leagues of land, which is equivalent to 48,708 acres. The result of the Mexican government's attempt to settle Texas by enticing Mexican citizens with vast land tracts was land speculation by Mexicans who purchased the land for themselves or on behalf of foreign investors. For example, the Galveston Bay Company, organized in 1830 and owned by North Americans, had title to 204,216 acres of land in Texas which three Mexican *empresarios* had purchased and then sold to the company. See C. Allan Hutchinson, "General José Antonio Mexía and his Texas Interests," *Southwestern Historical Quarterly* 80 (October 1978): 117–142.
40. Foote, *Texas*, 224.
41. Red, *The Texas Colonists*, 24.
42. Ibid., 14.
43. Ibid., 25.
44. Ibid., 26.
45. Ibid., 27. [Emphasis mine.]
46. Ibid.
47. Benson, "Texas as Viewed from Mexico," 245.
48. Priestly, *The Mexican Nation*, 280.
49. Ibid.
50. Ibid.
51. Benson, "Texas as Viewed from Mexico," 265.
52. Ibid.
53. Miller, "Austin and the Anglo-Texan Response," 299.
54. Priestly, *The Mexican Nation*, 281.
55. McKnight, "Austin's Legalistic Concerns," 256.
56. Hutchinson, "General José Antonio Mexía," 128.
57. Red, *The Texas Colonists*, 31.
58. Ibid., 30.
59. Priestly, *The Mexican Nation*, 282.
60. Ibid., 283.
61. Ibid., 283–284.
62. McKnight, "Austin's Legalistic Concerns," 264.
63. Priestly, *The Mexican Nation*, 284.
64. Historians have sought to explain the many forces at work that produced the Texas rebellion during the period in which the Mexican government was internally weakened by its own power struggles. Unpopular immigration laws; widespread dissatisfaction with the creation of the state of Coahuila y Texas; blunders in political calculations about the dynamic surge into the Texas borderlands by North American settlers; even conspiracy theo-

ries such as the scheming between Andrew Jackson and Sam Houston, are some of the issues that have been examined. For more literature on this period of Mexican-Texan history please see Benson, "Texas as Viewed from Mexico, 1820–1834," 219–291; Carlos E. Castañeda, trans., *The Mexican Side of the Texas Revolution* (Dallas, Tex.: P. L. Turner, 1928); and Hutchinson, "General José Antonio Mexia," 117–142. For an examination of the conspiracy theory see, Richard R. Stenberg, "The Texas Schemes of Jackson and Houston, 1829–1836," *Southwestern Social Science Quarterly* 15 (December 1934): 229–250.

65. De León, *Mexican Americans in Texas*, 29.

66. Ibid., 30.

67. Weber, *Myth and the History of the Hispanic Southwest*, 138.

68. Ibid., 139.

69. De León, *Mexican Americans in Texas*, 31.

70. Ibid.

71. Ibid., 32.

72. Miller, "Austin and the Anglo-Texan Response," 287.

73. Ibid.

74. Red, *The Texas Colonists*, 32.

75. Ibid.

76. Gilbert Hinojosa, "The Enduring Hispanic Faith Communities: Spanish and Texas Church Historiography," *The Journal of Texas Catholic History and Culture* 22 (March 1990): 35.

77. Ibid., 29.

78. The issue of the effectiveness of the Roman Catholic Church in the Texas borderlands (and elsewhere in the Southwest) has led to some interesting debates. In "The Enduring Hispanic Faith Communities," Hinojosa argues that the normative historical stance has been that the Roman Catholic Church, first under Spain then under Mexico, was a failed enterprise, especially upon the collapse of the missions system. Hinojosa writes, "[The] emphasis on the classic mission system disregards the evangelization of the natives through other means, overlooks the life of faith in non-mission communities, and gives the impression that when the missions ceased to exist as institutions all the work of the Church also ended. . . . This lack of research on the local diocesan church (that is the communities of faith under the bishop's supervision) has produced the impression, accepted even by otherwise cautious historians, that the Church was not serving the Texas settlements adequately and that the Catholic faith was somehow defective and weak. . . . The new nineteenth-century communities, which included large numbers of foreign immigrants, were assigned priests, and the military units sent to the Texas frontier were served by chaplains. From all indications, then, the Church and the faith that sustained it were strong across the vast expanse of today's Texas" (26, 27, 30). Hinojosa's challenge is for research to be done in the diocesan archives taking into account "the socio-economic, political, and cultural contexts of those Indian-Hispanic—and eventually foreign—communities on the northern frontier" (34). Hinojosa is critical of the recent his-

torical work of David J. Weber (cf. Weber's "Failure of a Frontier Institution: The Secular Church in the Borderlands under Independent Mexico, 1821–1846" in *The Western Historical Quarterly* 12 (April 1981): 125–143; also, Weber's *The Mexican Frontier, 1821–1846*, 69–82) and other Borderlands historians whom he says have perpetuated a "caricatured history of the local Hispanic faith communities" (33).

79. An interesting historical footnote is the fact that in *The Mexican Frontier, 1821–1846* Weber points to the charges which were brought against Fathers Refugio de la Garza and José Antonio Valdéz by the citizens of their parishes for the years they neglected to "preach, hear confessions, say Mass on a regular basis, or attend the sick and dying" (77). While Weber admits that these charges were most likely exaggerations, his focus on the negatives of the Mexican borderlands church stands as evidence of the traditional historical focus which Hinojosa is so critical of.

80. Red, *The Texas Colonists*, 33.

81. Miller, "Austin and the Anglo-Texan Response," 303.

82. Ibid., 287.

83. Ibid., 284.

84. Ibid., 299.

85. Ibid.

86. Ibid., 300.

87. Letters written by Austin in 1822–1823 give witness to his anticlericalism. Austin described travel in Mexico as the encounter with a church and clergy which was "maintained in their sacrilegious abuses by the blindness and ignorance of a fanatical people" (quoted in Miller, 304). Austin was also especially critical of the regular clergy. He described the friars as the "enemies of liberty, human happiness and of the human race" (ibid., 304).

88. Red, *The Texas Colonists*, 73.

89. Ibid.

90. Ibid., 74.

91. Ibid.

92. Ibid., 75.

93. Ibid., 77.

94. Ibid., 80.

95. Ibid., 81.

96. Estep, "Religion in the Lone Star State," 181.

97. Colby Hall, *Texas Disciples* (Fort Worth: Texas Christian University Press, 1953), 37.

98. Carter E. Boren, *Early History of the Disciples in Texas* (Masters Thesis, University of Chicago, 1937), 5.

99. Hall, *Texas Disciples*, 38.

100. Miller, "Austin and the Anglo-Texan Response," 312.

101. Boren, *Early History of the Disciples*, 17.

102. Ibid., 19.

103. Ibid., 23.

104. Hall reports that two earlier congregations were started in Clarksville and Antioch in 1836 (*Texas Disciples,*)

105. Ibid., 39.

106. Ibid., 89.

107. Boren, *Early History of the Disciples*, 28. [Emphasis mine.]

108. Ibid., 75.

109. Ibid., 84.

110. Hall, *Texas Disciples*, 129.

111. Boren, *Early History*, 29.

Chapter Five

1. *Missionary Tidings* 6 (October 1888): 9.

2. Ibid.

3. "Mexican-Americans," *Survey of Service* (St. Louis, Mo.: Christian Board of Publication, 1928), 121.

4. J. C. Mason, "Annual Address of the Corresponding Secretary of the Texas Christian Missionary Board," *Texas Missions* 3 (June 1906): 12 (identifies "Y. Quintero" as Ignacio Quintero.).

5. Carter E. Boren, *Religion on the Texas Frontier* (San Antonio, Tex.: The Naylor Co., 1968), 184.

6. Ibid., 190.

7. Mason, "Annual Address," 8.

8. Ibid., 4–5.

9. Ibid., 12.

10. Ibid.

11. Ibid.

12. "Texas," *Texas Missions* 4 (January 1907): 17.

13. Mason, "Annual Address," 12.

14. "Texas," *Texas Missions* 4 (January 1907): 17.

15. "Coahuila and Texas Frontier," *Missionary Tidings* 30 (November 1912): 229. The Martindale mission is reported as under the leadership of "its elder, Lorenzo García, who is a most enthusiastic lay evangelist" (229).

16. The Lockhart mission is mentioned in the various articles in *Missionary Tidings* in 1912 and 1914 and then in the 1920–21 *Year Book*. The Martindale mission only appears in the 1907 article in *Texas Missions* and is absent from all other reports.

17. By 1920 the Disciples had established missions work in *San Luis Potosí*, *Aguascalientes*, *Zacatecas*, and *Monterrey*.

18. Elmira J. Dickinson, *Historical Sketch of the Christian Woman's Board of Missions* (Indianapolis, Ind.: Christian Woman's Board of Missions, 1911), 31.

19. Dickinson, 35.

20. *Texas* Missions 5 (August 1908): 7.

21. Dickinson reports that by 1908 "no meetings had been held for more than a year" (35) at the San Antonio Mexican Mission. This would mean that Ignacio Quintero served this Tejano church start in San Antonio from 1899 to 1907.

22. *Survey of Service*, 121–122.

23. In *Texas Missions* 4 (February 1907): 5, there is a picture of "Mexican workers" in which can be found F. B. Jiménez and Manuel Lozano.

24. "Christian Women's Board of Missions," *Official Program of the International Missionary Convention*, October 9–15, 1908: 11.

25. *Texas Missions* 2 (October 1905): 6. [Emphasis mine.]

26. "Church Work in Border Towns," *World Call* 2 (February 1920): 41.

27. "Coahuila and Texas Frontier," *Missionary Tidings* 30 (November 1912): 229. The five churches listed are: Lockhart (Pastor Julian Salinas), San Antonio (Pastor Manuel Lozano), Martindale (Lorenzo García, lay preacher), Sabinal (Pastor José López, student from Mexico, assigned for summer 1912), and San Benito (Pastor Mauricio Alonzo, another student who served only as preacher and baptized new converts in 1912) (229). [Emphasis mine.]

28. "Mexico," *Missionary Tidings* 30 (May 1912): 27.

29. *Missionary Tidings* 32 (November 1914): 291.

30. "Coahuila and Texas Frontier," *Missionary Tidings* 30 (November 1912): 229.

31. "Mexican Work in Texas," *Missionary Tidings* 32 (November 1914): 291.

32. "Other Mexican Churches, *Missionary Tidings* 34 (November 1916): 274.

33. Blanche B. De Vore, *Land and Liberty: A History of the Mexican Revolution* (New York: Pageant Press, Inc., 1966), provides a clear examination of the complex issues involving the distribution of the land, and the many Spanish as well as Mexican land laws, which led to this bloody period of Mexican history.

34. See Deborah J. Baldwin, *Protestants and the Mexican Revolution, Missionaries, Ministers, and Social Change* (Urbana: University of Illinois Press, 1990).

35. "Other Mexican Churches," *Missionary Tidings* 34 (November 1916): 274.

36. Byron Spice, in his book *Discípulos Americanos: Sixty-five Years of Christian Churches' Ministry to Spanish Speaking Persons* (Indianapolis: United Christian Missionary Society, 1964), gives information that differs from the articles that appeared in *Missionary Tidings* as well as *Year Book* information. Spice says Pilar Silva continued in San Benito "until 1924" and that "the was revived again in 1929 by Glen H. Tussing. Since then, several ministers have led the church" (49). There are no *Year Book* listings for this church throughout the 1920s, and no mention is made of it any of the missionary news-

papers. Glen Tussing does indeed appear listed as pastor of the San Benito mission from 1931 to 1932. The next mention of a pastor serving in San Benito is in the 1935 *Year Book* and the name given is Fred Vásquez, who served until 1939.

37. "Other Mexican Churches," *Missionary Tidings* 34 (November 1916): 274.

38. "Mexican Work," *Missionary Tidings* 34 (December 1916): 323.

39. "Other Mexican Churches," *Missionary Tidings* 34 (November 1916): 274.

40. The number of Mexican immigrants coming into the U.S. borderlands during this time of revolution was further increased by the proximity of the U.S. border, the U.S. asylum policy, and the U.S. wartime need for *braceros*. See Lawrence A. Cardoso, *Mexican Emigration to the United States, 1897–1931* (Tucson: University of Arizona Press, 1980).

41. E. T. Cornelius, "Mexicans in the United States," *World Call* 1 (September 1919): 29–31. [Emphasis mine.]

42. "Mexicans in the United States," *World Call* 2 (November 1920): 48.

43. *Missionary Tidings* 30 (February, 1913): 389.

44. *Survey of Service*, 124.

45. *Missionary Tidings* 32 (November 1914): 291.

46. Ibid.

47. *Survey of Service*, 127. [Emphasis mine.]

48. *Missionary Tidings* 32 (October 1914): 218.

49. *Missionary Tidings* 32 (November 1914): 291.

50. "Spanish-American and Mexican Work in the United States," *Year Book* (October 1920–June 1921): 90. This report mentions that "two small churches were united into one church" to form the reorganized Mexican Church in 1920. No other records for when and where this second Disciples mission in San Antonio was started have been found.

51. Ibid., 90.

52. "Mexican-Americans," *Survey of Service* (St. Louis, Mo.: Christian Board of Publication, 1928), 123.

53. Ibid.

54. United Christian Missionary Society, *Year Book* (October 1920–June 1921) (St. Louis, Mo.: United Christian Missionary Society, 1921), 90–91.

55. United Christian Missionary Society, *Year Book* (October 1920–June 1921) (St. Louis, Mo.: United Christian Missionary Society, 1921), 91.

56. United Christian Missionary Society, *Year Book* (July 1923–June 1924) (St. Louis, Mo.: United Christian Missionary Society, 1924), 99–100.

57. *Survey of Service*, 120–130.

58. Byron Spice, *Discípulos Americanos*, 51.

59. Ibid., 50–51.

60. Ibid., 50.

61. Ibid. 51.

62. Ibid.

63. Colby Hall is the only writer who mentions two "Latin American" people who graduated from Texas Christian University and then stayed to serve in Texas (408).

64. The 1924 *Year Book*, lists Pablo Gloria as working in Fort Worth that year. The church is listed in the years 1925 and 1926 after which it is not mentioned again. Fred Vásquez is first listed in the *Year Books* for 1935–1945 as pastor in San Benito.

65. Campbell's early interest in the peace movement is reflected in articles written as early as 1834. See *Millennial Harbinger* 5 (July 1834): 306–309. Harold L. Lunger, in his book, *The Political Ethics of Alexander Campbell* (St. Louis, Mo.: The Bethany Press, 1954), provides a good examination of Campbell's pacifism; see pp. 242–257.

66. "War," *Millennial Harbinger* 3 (November 1846): 638–642.

67. Ibid.

68. Ibid., 638 ff.

69. Ibid. [Emphasis mine.]

70. The issue of slavery was one Alexander Campbell wrote about extensively. He took an antislavery stand, but his concerns and arguments changed in response to the realities of the nation and his own evolving thought. See Lunger, *Political Ethics*, 193–232, for a good analysis of Campbell's treatment of the slave issue.

71. For an example of Campbell's ideas about the United States prior to the Mexican-American War, see "An Oration in Honor of the Fourth of July, 1830," in *Popular Lectures and Addresses* (Cincinnati, Ohio: Central Book Concern, 1879), 367–378.

72. Lunger, *Political Ethics*, 152–154.

73. Ibid., 152–154.

74. Alexander Campbell, "Importance of Uniting the Moral with the Intellectual Culture of the Mind," *Popular Lectures and Addresses* (Cincinnati, Ohio: Central Book Concern, 1879), 453–484.

75. Lunger, *Political Ethics*, 157.

76. David E. Harrell, Jr., *Quest for a Christian America: The Disciples of Christ and American Society to 1866* (Nashville, Tenn.: The Disciples of Christ Historical Society, 1966), 140.

77. Robert Forrester, "The War," *Protestant Unionist* 2 (November 18, 1846): 198; quoted in David E. Harrell, Jr., *Quest for a Christian America: The Disciples of Christ and American Society to 1866* (Nashville, Tenn.: The Disciples of Christ Historical Society, 1966), 142.

78. See Colby Hall, *Texas Disciples* (Fort Worth: Texas Christian University Press, 1953), 64–74.

79. *Year Book* 1906, 500; quoted in Carter E. Boren, *Religion on the Texas Frontier* (San Antonio, Tex.: The Naylor Co., 1968), 61.

80. Boren, *Religion on the Texas Frontier*, 160.

81. Ibid., 159.

82. Campbell had addressed this issue in the 13th Proposition of his *Dec-

laration and Address which he wrote in 1809. Campbell stated, "if any circumstances indispensably necessary to the observance of the Divine ordinances be not found upon the page of express revelation, such . . . as are only necessary for this purpose should be adopted under the title human expedients, without any pretense to a more sacred origin, so that any subsequent alteration or difference in the observance of these things might produce no contention or division in the Church." Quoted in Hall, *Texas Disciples*, 136.

83. Boren in *Religion on the Texas Frontier*, states: "Almost every preacher for the Disciples in Texas came from Kentucky, and those who did not were principally from Mississippi, Alabama, and Tennessee" (30).

84. Ibid., 86.

85. An interesting example of how much strife there was is an incident that occurred in late 1893 or early 1894. T. B. Larrimore, a representative of the conservative church newspaper *Gospel Advocate,* conducted a revival at the Sherman Texas Disciples church. Though he advocated a "non-organ position" (he would preach even if there was an organ), six months after the revival the organ was removed. When the progressive members tried to replace the organ, they were locked out of the building, which led to a lawsuit being filed for possession of the church building in June 1894. See Boren, *Religion in the Texas Frontier*, for court minutes (120–129).

86. See Boren, *Religion on the Texas Frontier*, for a detailed account of some of the congregations that experienced division. His use of congregational minutes and court proceedings makes for an interesting narrative of the internal tensions among Texas Disciples (106–134).

87. Ibid., 142–145.

88. Ibid., 142.

89. Ibid., 144.

Conclusion

1. The first overseas Disciples missionary was Dr. James Turner Barclay, who arrived in Jerusalem on February 8, 1851. He was sent by the newly formed American Christian Missionary Society (org. in 1849), whose first president was Alexander Campbell.

2. In the state of Indiana, German "Dunkard" churches became a part of the Disciples movement. See Henry K. Shaw, *Hoosier Disciples* (St. Louis, Mo.: The Bethany Press, 1966).

3. Boren, *Religion on the Texas Frontier*, 340.

4. Ibid., 160.

5. See David Montejanos, *Anglos and Mexicans in the Making of Texas* (Austin: University of Texas Press, 1989), who gives an excellent analysis of the relation between race and land ownership and the displacement of the Tejanos from their own land (74–99). Montejano makes this comment about the relation between race and economic factors: "In the late nineteenth cen-

tury, these [Anglo-Mexican] race sentiments, which drew heavily from the legacy of the Alamo and the Mexican War, were maintained and sharpened by market competition and property disputes" (82). It would be inaccurate to think that Disciples in Texas, who were also trying to make their living, would not have been affected by the connections Montejano examines between economic advancement in Texas and the issue of race.

6. Boren, *Religion on the Texas Frontier*, 339.

Bibliography

Books

Abalos, David T. *Latinos in the United States: The Sacred and the Profane.* Notre Dame, Ind.: University of Notre Dame Press, 1986.

Acuña, Rodolfo. *Occupied America: A History of Chicanos.* San Francisco, Calif.: Canfield Press, 1972.

Ahlstrom, Sydney. *A Religious History of the American People.* New Haven, Conn.: Yale University Press, 1972.

Alvear Acevedo, Carlos. *Historia de México.* México: Editorial Jus, 1964.

Anaya, Rodolfo A., and Francisco Lomeli, eds. *Aztlán: Essays on the Chicano Homeland.* Albuquerque: University of New Mexico Press, 1989.

Baldwin, Deborah J. *Protestants and the Mexican Revolution, Missionaries, Ministers and Social Change.* Urbana: University of Illinois Press, 1990.

Bannon, John F., ed. *Bolton and the Spanish Borderlands.* Norman: University of Oklahoma Press, 1964.

Barrera, Mario. *Race and Class in the Southwest: A Theory of Racial Inequality.* Notre Dame, Ind.: University of Notre Dame Press, 1979.

Bean, Frank D., and Marta Tienda. *The Hispanic Population of the United States.* New York: Russell Sage Foundation, 1987.

Beazley, George R., ed. *The Christian Church (Disciples of Christ): An Interpretive Examination in the Cultural Context.* St. Louis, Mo.: The Bethany Press, 1973

———. "Who Are the Disciples?" In *The Christian Church (Disciples of Christ): An Interpretative Examination in the Cultural Context*, ed. George E. Beazley, Jr. St. Louis, Mo.: The Bethany Press, 1973.

Bennett, James D. *Frederick Jackson Turner.* Boston, Mass.: Twayne, 1975.

Benson, Lee. "The Historian as Mythmaker: Turner and the Closed Frontier." In *The Frontier in American Development: Essays in Honor of Paul Wallace Gates,* ed. David M. Ellis. Ithaca, N.Y.: University of Cornell Press, 1969.

Billington, Ray Allen, ed. *Frontier and Section, Selected: Essays of Frederick Jackson Turner.* Englewood Cliffs, N.J.: Prentice-Hall, 1961.

Bolton, Herbert E. *The Spanish Borderlands, A Chronicle of Old Florida and the Southwest.* New Haven, Conn.: Yale University Press, 1921.

———. *Wider Horizons of American History.* New York: D. Appleton Century, 1939.

Boren, Carter E. *Religion on the Texas Frontier.* San Antonio, Tex.: The Naylor Co., 1968.

Boring, Eugene. "The Disciples and Higher Criticism: The Crucial Third Generation." In *A Case Study in Mainstream Protestantism,* ed. D. Newell Williams. Grand Rapids, Mich.: Eerdmans, 1991.

Brackenridge, R. Douglas, and Francisco Gracía-Treto. *Iglesia Presbiteriana: A History of Presbyterians and Mexican Americans in the Southwest.* San Antonio, Tex.: Trinity University Press, 1987.

Brown, Charles H. *Agents of Manifest Destiny.* Chapel Hill: University of North Carolina Press, 1980.

Buckner, Alice G., Lyle V. Newman, and Ruth Estes Milner. *Disciples of Christ and Spanish-Speaking Americans: A Symposium.* Indianapolis, Ind.: The United Christian Missionary Society, 1953.

Buenger, Walter L., and Robert A. Calvert, eds. *Texas History and The Move into the Twenty-First Century.* Austin: Texas Committee for the Humanities, 1990.

———. *Texas Through Time, Evolving Interpretations.* College Station: Texas A & M University Press, 1991.

Campbell, Alexander. *The Christian System in Reference to the Union of Christians and Restoration of Primitive Christianity.* 2d ed. Pittsburgh, Pa.: Forrester & Campbell, 1839.

———. *Popular Lectures and Addresses.* Cincinnati, Ohio: Central Book Concern, 1879.

Cardoso, Lawrence. *Mexican Emigration to the United States, 1897–1931.* Tucson: University of Arizona Press, 1980.

Carrasco, David. *Religions of Mesoamerica.* San Francisco: Harper & Row, 1990.

Castleman, William J. *Samuel Guy Inman, 1905–1916,* vol. 2. Indianapolis, Ind.: Christian Communications Reporter, 1969.

Chipman, Donald E. "Spanish Texas." In *Texas Through Time: Evolving Interpretations,* ed. Walter L. Buenger and Robert A. Calvert. College Station: Texas A & M University Press, 1991.

Crain, James A. *The Development of Social Ideas Among the Disciples of Christ.* St. Louis, Mo.: The Bethany Press, 1969.

Cutler, Wayne, John S. D. Eisenhower, Miguel E. Soto, and Douglas W. Richmond. *Essays on the Mexican War.* College Station: Texas A & M University Press, 1986.

De León, Arnoldo. *They Called Them Greasers: Anglo Attitudes Towards Mexicans in Texas, 1821–1900.* Austin: University of Texas Press, 1983.

———. "Texas Mexicans: Twentieth Century Interpretations." In *Texas Through Time, Evolving Interpretations,* ed. Walter L. Buenger and Robert A. Calvert. College Station: Texas A & M University Press, 1991.

———. *Mexican Americans in Texas: A Brief History.* Arlington Heights, Ill.: Harlan Davidson, Inc., 1993.

Department of Commerce and Labor, Bureau of Statistics. *Religious Bodies: 1906.* Washington, D.C.: Government Printing Office, 1910.

De Vore, Blanche. *Land and Liberty: A History of the Mexican Revolution.* New York: Pageant Press, Inc., 1966.

Drinnon, Richard. *Facing West: The Metaphysics of Indian-Hating and Empire Building.* Minneapolis: University of Minnesota Press, 1980.

Fehrenbach, T. R. *Lone Star: A History of Texas and the Texans.* New York: Macmillan, 1968.

Foote, Henry Stuart. *Texas and the Texans.* Philadelphia, Pa.: Thomas, Copperthwait & Co., 1841; reprint, Austin: The Steck Company, 1935.

Fuentes Mares, José. *Génesis del expansionismo norteamericano.* México, D.F.: El Colegio de México, 1980.

Gabriel, Ralph Henry. *The Lure of The Frontier: A Story of Race Conflict.* New Haven, Conn.: Yale University Press, 1929.

García Cantú, Gastón. *La idea de México*, vol. I, *Los Estados Unidos.* México, D.F.: Fondo de Cultura Económica, 1991.

Garrison, Winfred Ernest. *Religion Follows the Frontier: A History of the Disciples of Christ.* New York: Harper & Brothers, 1931.

———. and A.T. DeGroot. *The Disciples of Christ: A History.* St. Louis, Mo.: The Bethany Press, 1948.

Gilpin, Clark W. "Faith on the Frontier: Historical Interpretations of the Disciples of Christ." In *A Case Study of Mainstream Protestantism*, ed. D. Newell Williams. St. Louis, Mo.: Chalice Press, 1991.

Goetzmann, William H. *Exploration and Empire.* New York: W. W. Norton, 1966.

González, Justo L., ed. *Each in Our Own Tongue: A History of Hispanic United Methodism.* Nashville, Tenn.: Abingdon Press, 1991.

Graebner, Norman, ed. *Manifest Destiny.* Indianapolis: Bobbs-Merrill, 1968.

Griswold del Castillo, Richard. *The Treaty of Guadalupe Hidalgo: A Legacy of Conflict.* Norman: University of Oklahoma Press, 1990.

Hall, Colby D. *Texas Disciples.* Fort Worth: Texas Christian University Press, 1953.

Handy, Robert T. *A History of the Churches in the United States and Canada.* Oxford: Oxford University Press, 1976.

Hanke, Lewis. *Aristotle and the American Indian*. Bloomington: Indiana University Press, 1959.

———. *The First Social Experiments in America*. Gloucester, Mass.: Peter Smith, 1964.

Harrell, David E., Jr. *Quest for a Christian America: The Disciples of Christ and American Society to 1866*. Nashville, Tenn.: The Disciples of Christ Historical Society, 1966.

———. *The Social Sources of Division in the Disciples of Christ, 1865–1900*. Atlanta, Ga.: Publishing Systems, 1973.

Hietala, Thomas R. *Manifest Design: Anxious Aggrandizement in Late Jacksonian America*. Ithaca, N.Y.: University of Cornell Press, 1958.

Horsman, Reginald. *Race and Manifest Destiny*. Cambridge: Harvard University Press, 1981.

Hudson, Winthrop S. *Religion in America: An Historical Account of the Development of American Religious Life*. New York: Charles Scribner's Sons, 1973.

Hughes, Richard T., ed. *The American Quest for the Primitive Church*. Urbana: University of Illinois Press, 1988.

———. *The Primitive Church in the Modern World*. Urbana: University of Illinois Press, 1995.

Humble, Bill J. *Campbell and Controversy*. Joplin, Mo.: College Press, 1986.

Inman, Samuel Guy. *Christian Cooperation in Latin America*. New York: Committee on Cooperation in Latin America, 1917.

———. *Intervention in Mexico*. New York: Association Press, 1919.

———. *Conferencias dadas a la Universidad Nacional de México*. México, D.F.: Talleres Gráficos, 1927.

———. *América Revolucionaria: Conferencia y ensayos*, ed Javier Morata. Madrid: 1933.

Jacobs, Wilbur R., John W. Caughey, and Joe B. Frantz. *Turner, Bolton, and Webb: Three Historians of the American Frontier*. Seattle: University of Washington Press, 1965.

Jay, William. *A Review of the Causes and Consequences of the Mexican War*. 1849; reprint, Freeport: Books for Libraries Press, 1970.

Jehlen, Myra. *American Incarnation: The Individual, The Nation, The Continent*. Cambridge, Mass.: Harvard University Press, 1986.

Jewett, Robert. *The Captain America Complex, The Dilemma of Zealous Nationalism*. Philadelphia, Pa.: Westminster Press, 1973.

Jiménez, Alfredo, ed. *Handbook of Hispanic Cultures in the United States: History*. Houston, Tex.: Arte Público Press, 1994.

Jones, Oakah L., Jr. *Los Paisanos: Spanish Settlers on the Northern Frontier of New Spain*. Norman: University of Oklahoma Press, 1979.

———. *Nueva Vizcaya, Heartland of the Spanish Frontier*. Albuquerque: University of New Mexico Press, 1988.

Lack, Paul D. "In the Long Shadow of Eugene C. Barker: The Revolution and the Republic." In *Texas Through Time: Evolving Interpretations*, ed.

Walter L. Buenger and Robert A. Calvert. College Station: Texas A & M University Press, 1991.

Langum, David J. "Herbert Eugene Bolton." In *Historians of the American Frontier*, ed. John R. Wunder. New York: Greenwood Press, 1988.

Limerick, Patricia N., Clyde A. Milner II, and Charles E. Rankin, eds. *Trails: Towards a New Western History*. Lawrence: University of Kansas Press, 1991.

Lunger, Harold L. *The Political Ethics of Alexander Campbell*. St. Louis, Mo.: The Bethany Press, 1954.

Luzbetak, Louis T. *The Church and Cultures: New Perspectives in Missiological Anthropology*. Maryknoll, N.Y.: Orbis Books, 1988.

Marty, Martin E. *Pilgrims In Their Own Land: 500 Years of Religion in America*. Boston, Mass.: Little, Brown, 1984.

———. *Religion and Republic*. Boston, Mass.: Beacon Press, 1987.

McAllister, Lester, ed. *An Alexander Campbell Reader*. St. Louis, Mo.: Christian Board of Publication, 1988.

———. and William E. Tucker. *Journey in Faith: A History of the Christian Church (Disciples of Christ)*. St. Louis, Mo.: The Bethany Press, 1975.

Merk, Frederick. *Manifest Destiny and Mission in American History: A Reinterpretation*. New York: Alfred A. Knopf, 1963.

———. *The Monroe Doctrine and American Expansionism, 1843–1849*. New York: Alfred A, Knopf, 1966.

Montejano, David. *Anglos and Mexicans in the Making of Texas*. Austin: University of Texas Press, 1989.

Moore, William Thomas. *A Comprehensive History of the Disciples of Christ*. New York: Fleming H. Revell, 1909.

Moseley, J. Edward, ed. *The Spanish-Speaking People of the Southwest*. Council on Spanish-American Work, 1966.

Nash, Roderick. *Wilderness and the American Mind*. 3d ed. New Haven, Conn.: Yale University Press, 1982.

Niebuhr, H. Richard. *Christ and Culture*. New York: Harper & Row, 1951.

———. "The Protestant Movement and Democracy in the United States." In *Religion in American Life*, vol. 1: *The Shaping of America*, ed. James Ward Smith and A. Leland Jamison. Princeton, N.J.: Princeton University Press, 1961.

———. *The Kingdom of God in America*. Middletown, Conn.: Wesleyan University Press, 1988.

Noble, David W. *Historians Against History: The Frontier Thesis and the National Covenant in American Historical Writing since 1830*. Minneapolis: University of Minnesota Press, 1965.

O'Gorman, Edmundo. *The Invention of America: An Inquiry into the Historical Nature of the New World and the Meaning of Its History*. Bloomington: Indiana University Press, 1961.

Osborn, Ronald E. "Theology Among the Disciples." In *The Christian Church (Disciples of Christ): An Interpretive Examination in the Cul-*

tural Context, ed. George E. Beazley. St. Louis, Mo.: The Bethany Press, 1975.

———. *Experiment in Liberty: The Ideal of Freedom in the Experience of the Disciples of Christ.* St. Louis, Mo.: The Bethany Press, 1978.

Powell, Philip Wayne. *Tree of Hate: Propaganda and Prejudices Affecting the United States' Relationships with the Hispanic World.* New York: Basic Books, 1971.

Poyo, Gilbert E., and Gilberto M. Hinojosa. *Tejano Origins in Eighteenth-Century San Antonio.* Austin: University of Texas Press, 1991.

Prago, Albert. *Strangers in Their Own Land, A History of Mexican Americans.* New York: Four Winds Press, 1973.

Price, Glenn W. *Origins of the War with Mexico.* Austin: University of Texas Press, 1967.

Priestly, Herbert I. *The Mexican Nation: A History.* New York: Macmillan, 1938.

Red, William Stuart. *The Texas Colonists and Religion 1821–1836.* Austin, Tex.: E. L. Shettles, Publisher 1924.

Rendón, Armando B. *Chicano Manifiesto.* New York: Macmillan, 1971.

Richey, Russell, and Donald G. Jones, eds. *American Civil Religion.* New York: Harper & Row, 1974.

Riding, Alan. *Distant Neighbors: A Portrait of the Mexicans.* New York: Vintage Books, 1984.

Robinson, Cecil. *With The Ears of Strangers: The Mexican in American Literature.* Tucson: University of Arizona Press, 1963.

———. *Mexico and the Hispanic Southwest in American Literature.* Tucson: University of Arizona Press, 1977.

Rodríguez, Daniel, and David Cortés. *Hidden Stories: Unveiling the History of the Latino Church.* Decatur, Ga.: Asociación para la Educación Teológica Hispana, 1994.

Rosenbaum, Robert J. *Mexicano Resistance in the Southwest.* Austin: University of Texas Press, 1981.

Sandoval, Moisés, ed. *Fronteras: A History of the Latin American Church in the USA Since 1513.* San Antonio, Tex.: Mexican American Cultural Center, 1983.

———. *On The Move: A History of the Hispanic Church in the United States.* Maryknoll, N.Y.: Orbis Books, 1991.

Simmen, Edward, ed. *The Chicano: From Caricature to Self-Portrait.* New York: New American Library, 1971.

Smith, Jesse Guy. *Heroes of the Saddle Bags: A History of Christian Denominations in The Republic of Texas.* San Antonio, Tex.: The Naylor Co., 1951.

Spice, Byron. *Discípulos Americanos: Sixty-five Years of Christian Churches' Ministry to Spanish-Speaking Persons.* Indianapolis, Ind.: United Christian Missionary Society, 1964.

———. *Report on The Spanish Work Consultation, May 9–13, 1966.* Indianapolis, Ind.: Department of Home Mission Ministries.

Stump, Roger W. "Spatial Patterns of Growth and Decline among the Disciples of Christ, 1890–1980." In *Case Study of Mainstream Protestantism,* ed. D. Newell Williams. Grand Rapids, Mich.: Eerdmans, 1991.

Sweet, William W. *The Story of Religion in America.* New York: Harper, 1939.

———. *Religion on the American Frontier, 1783–1840.* Chicago, Ill.: The University of Chicago Press, 1946.

———. *Religion in the Development of America Culture, 1765–1840.* New York: Scribner's Sons, 1952.

Takaki, Ronald. *A Different Mirror: A History of Multicultural America.* Boston, Mass.: Little, Brown, 1993.

Taylor, Paul S. *An American-Mexican Frontier.* New York: Russell & Russell, 1934.

Teegarden, Kenneth. *We Call Ourselves Disciples.* St. Louis, Mo.: The Bethany Press, 1975.

Todorov, Tzvetan. *The Conquest of America.* New York: Harper & Row, 1987.

Turner, Frederick Jackson. *The Significance of the Frontier in American History.* State Historical Society of Wisconsin, 1893; reprint, El Paso, Tex.: Academic Reprints, 1960.

———. *The Problem of the West.* In *Frontier and Section: Selected Essays of Frederick Jackson Turner.* With an introduction by Ray Allen Billington. Englewood Cliffs, N.J.: Prentice-Hall, 1961.

United Christian Missionary Society. *1920–21 Year Book ; 1924 Year Book (July 1923– June 30, 1924); 1930—1945 Year Books.* St. Louis, Mo.: United Christian Missionary Society, 1921; 1924; 1930–1945.

United Christian Missionary Society. *Survey of Service.* St. Louis, Mo.: Christian Board of Publication, 1928.

Weber, David J. *The Mexican Frontier, 1821–1846.* Albuquerque: Unviersity of New Mexico Press, 1982.

———. *Myth and the History of the Hispanic Southwest.* Albuquerque: University of New Mexico Press, 1988.

———. *The Spanish Frontier in North America.* New Haven, Conn.: Yale University Press, 1992.

Weber, David J., ed. *Foreigners In Their Native Land: Historical Roots of the Mexican Americans.* Albuquerque: University of New Mexico Press, 1973.

———. *Northern Mexico on the Eve of the United States Invasion.* New York: Arno Press, 1976.

———. *New Spain's Far Northern Frontier.* Albuquerque: University of New Mexico Press, 1979.

Weinberg, Albert K. *Manifest Destiny: A Study of Nationalist Expansionism in American History.* Gloucester, Mass.: Peter Smith, 1958.

West, Robert F. *Alexander Campbell and Natural Religion.* New Haven, Conn.: Yale University Press, 1948.

Weston, Rubin Francis. *Racism in United States Imperialism: The Influence of Racial Assumptions on American Foreign Policy, 1893–1946.* Columbia: University of South Carolina Press, 1972.

Weyer, Thomas. *Hispanic U.S.A.: Breaking the Melting Pot.* New York: Harper & Row, 1988.

Wolf, Eric R. *Europe and the People Without History.* Berkeley: University of California Press, 1982.

Wood, Forrest G. *The Arrogance of Faith: Christianity and Race in America from the Colonial Era to the Twentieth Century.* New York: Alfred A. Knopf, 1990.

Worcester, Donald E. "The Significance of the Spanish Borderlands to the United States." In *New Spain's Far Northern Frontier*, ed. David J. Weber. Albuquerque: University of New Mexico Press, 1979.

Wunder, John, R., ed. *Historians of the American Froniter.* New York: Greenwood Press, 1988.

Yoakum, H. *History of Texas from Its First Settlement in 1685 to Its Annexation to the United States in 1846*, vol. 1. New York: Redfield, 1855; reprint, Austin, Tex.: Steck-Vaughn, no date.

Articles

Alamaraz, Felix D. "The Warp and the Weft: An Overview of the Social Fabric of Mexican Texas." *East Texas Historical Journal* 27 (1989): 13–23.

Atwater, Anna R. "The Heart of Mexico." *World Call* 1 (May 1919): 49–51.

Baldwin, Deborah. "Broken Traditions: Mexican Revolutionaries and Protestant Allegiances." *The Americas* 40 (October 1983): 229–258.

Barton, Paul. "Function and Dysfunction: A Case Study of Mexican-American Methodists." *Apuntes* 2 (Summer 1994): 35–51.

Benson, Nettie Lee. "Texas as Viewed from Mexico, 1820–1834." *Southwestern Historical Quarterly* 90 (January 1987): 219–291.

Billington, Ray A. "Frederick Jackson Turner, Non-Western Historian." *Wisconsin Academy of Sciences, Arts and Letters, Transactions* 59 (1971): 7–21

Christian Evangelist. "Mexican Mission Work in the United States." 19 September 1929.

Christian Evangelist. "Splendid Representation in Spanish American Convention." 2 January 1930.

Cornelius, Edwin T. "Mexicans in the United States." *World Call* 1 (September 1919): 48.

———. "Mexico." *World Call* 1 (October 1919): 22.

———. "The New Field of the Disciples of Christ in Mexico." *World Call* 2 (April 1920): 14–15.

———. "Spanish Americans." *Christian Evangelist* 29 August 1929.

Estep, W. R. "Religion in the Lone Star State: An Historical Perspective." *International Review of Mission* 78 (April 1989): 180–186.

García, Mario T. "La Frontera: The Border as Symbol and Reality in Mexican-American Thought." *Mexican Studies/Estudios Mexicanos* 1 (Summer 1985): 195–225.

González de la Vara, Martín. "Nuevos estudios sobre el suroeste norteamericano." *Mexican Studies/Estudios Mexicanos* 8 (Winter 1992): 107–115.

González, Justo. "Hispanics in the United States." *Listening: A Journal of Religion and Culture* 27 (Winter 1992): 7–16.

Hinojosa, Gilberto M. "The Enduring Hispanic Faith Communities: Spanish and Texas Church Historiography." *The Journal of Texas Catholic History and Culture* 22 (March 1990): 27–38.

Hughes, Richard T. "From Primitive Church to Civil Religion: The Millenial Odyssey of Alexander Campbell." *American Academy of Religion Journal* 44 (March 1976): 87–103.

———. "Civil Religion, the Theology of the Republic, and the Free Church Tradition." *Journal of Church and State* 22 (Winter 1980): 75–87.

Hutchinson, C. Alan. "General José Antonio Mexía and His Texas Interests." *Southwestern Historical Quarterly* 82 (October 1978): 117–142.

Inman, Samuel G. "Shall There Be Intervention?" *World Call* 1 (September 1919): 64.

Koll, Karla. "Samuel Guy Inman: Venturer in Inter-American Friendship." *Union Seminary Quarterly Review* 42 (1988): 45–66.

Kopp, Lewis P. "Church Work in Border Towns." *World Call* 2 (February 1920): 41.

Lack, Paul D. "Slavery and the Texas Revolution." *Southwestern Historical Quarterly* 89 (October 1985): 181–202.

Lara-Braud, Jorge. "Hispanic Ministry: Fidelity to Christ."*Pacific Theological Review* 19 (Winter 1986): 5–14.

Lewis, Merrill E. "The Art of Frederick Jackson Turner." *Wisconsin Academy of Sciences, Arts and Letters, Transactions* 59 (1971): 23–32.

Lores, Rubén. "Manifest Destiny and the Missionary Enterprise." *Study Encounter* 9 (1975): 1–16.

Luna, E. G. "Our Christian Obligation to the Mexican." *Christian Evangelist* 11 March 1937.

Mason, J. C. "Annual Address of the Corresponding Secretary of the Texas Missionary Board." *Texas Missions* 6 June 1906.

McKnight, Joseph W. "Stephen Austin's Legalistic Concerns." *Southwestern Historical Quarterly* 89 (January 1986): 239–268.

Mead, Sidney E. "The Theology of the Republic and the Orthodox Mind." *American Academy of Religion Journal* 44 (March 1976): 105–113.

Miller, Howard. "Stephen F. Austin and the Anglo-Texan Response to the Religious Establishment in Mexico, 1821–1836." *Southwestern Historical Quarterly* 91 (January 1988): 283–316.

Millennial Harbinger. 3 (November 1846): 638.

Missionary Tidings. 6 (October 1888): 8–9; 30 (May 1912): 27; 30 (November 1912): 227–230; 30 (January 1913): 352; 30 (February 1913): 389; 30 (March 1913): 427; 32 (May 1914): 14; 32 (July 1914): 102; 32 (November 1914): 289–292; 33 (May 1915): 10; 33 (September 1915): 168; 33 (November 1915): 277–279; 34 (Novmeber 1916): 271–275; 34 (December 1916): 323; 35 (October 1917): 210; 36 (June 1918): 51.

Morrison Michael A. "'New Territory vs. No Territory': The Whig Party and the Politics of Western Expansion, 1846–1848." *Western Historical Quarterly* 23 (February 1992): 25–51.

Nackman, Mark E. "Anglo-American Migrants to the West: Men of Broken Fortunes? The Case of Texas, 1821–1846." *Western Historical Quarterly* 5 (October 1974): 441–455.

Official Program of the International Missionary Convention, New Orleans, October 9–15, 1908: 11–13.

Pomeroy, Earl. "Toward a Reorientation of Western History: Continuity and Enviornment." *Mississippi Valley Historical Review* 41 (March 1955): 579–600.

Poyo, Gerald E., and Gilberto M. Hinojosa. "Spanish Texas and Borderlands Historiography in Transition: Implications for United States History." *The Journal of American History* 75 (September 1988): 393–416.

Putnam, Jackson K. "The Turner Thesis and the Westward Movement: An Appraisal." *Western Historical Quarterly* 7 (October 1976): 377–404.

Rivera-Pagán, Luis. "A New World and A New Church." *Conversations* 14 (Spring 1991): 16–20.

Segovia, Fernando F. "Two Places and No Place in Which to Stand: Mixture and Otherness in Hispanic American Theology." *Listening, a Journal of Religion and Culture* 27 (Winter 1992): 26–40.

Stagner, Stephen. "Epics, Science, and the Lost Frontier: Texas Historical Writing, 1836–1936." *Western Historical Quarterly* 12 (April 1981): 165–181.

Vázquez, Josefina Zoraida. "The Texas Question in Mexican Politics, 1836–1845." *Southwestern Historical Quarterly* 89 (January 1986): 309–344.

Texas Missions (Dallas). March, September, October 1907; August, November 1908.

Weber, David J. "Mexico's Far Northern Frontier, 1821–1854: Historiography Askew." *Western Historical Quarterly* 7 (July 1976): 279–293.

———. "Failure of a Frontier Institution: The Secular Church in the Borderlands under Independent Mexico, 1821–1846." *Western Historical Quarterly* 12 (April 1981): 125–143.

———. "The Spanish Legacy in North America and the Historical Imagination." *Western Historical Quarterly* 23 (1992): 5–24.

Worcester, Donald E. "The Significance of the Spanish Borderlands to the United States." *Western Historical Quarterly* 7 (January 1976): 5–18.

World Call 1 (December 1919): 8–10.

World Call 2 (November 1920): 48.

Unpublished Works

Boren, Carter E. *Early History of the Disciples of Christ in Texas*. Master's thesis, University of Chicago, 1937.

De León, Arnoldo. *White Racial Attitudes Toward Mexicanos In Texas, 1821–1900*. Ph.D. diss., Texas Christian University, 1974.

Gannett, William B. *The American Invasion of Texas, 1820–1845: Patterns of Conflict Between Settlers and Indians*. Ph.D diss., Cornell University, 1984.

Tijerina, Andrew A. *Tejanos and Texas: The Native Mexicans of Texas, 1820–1850*. Ph.D diss., University of Texas at Austin, 1977.

Wallace, Charles Ross. *Hispanic Disciples of Christ in the Christian Church (Disciples of Christ) Tradition*. Master's Thesis, Lexington Theological Seminary, 1989.

Index